The Secret of
Jewish Femininity

The Secret of Jewish Femininity

Insights into the Practice of

Taharat HaMishpachah

Tehilla Abramov

First Published 1988
New Edition 2005
Copyright © 2005 by Tehilla Abramov
ISBN 1-56871-351-7

Published by:
Jewish Marriage Education
POB 43206 Jerusalem, 91431 Israel
www.JewishFamily.org

Printed in Israel

This book was written in consultation with Maran HaGaon HaRav Shlomo Zalman Auerbach, *zt"l*. Maran HaGaon HaRav Yosef Sholom Elyashiv, *shlita*, was consulted on some matters.

The whole book was reviewed by Maran HaGaon HaRav Shlomo Zalman Auerbach, *zt"l*, who approved of all the halachot in the book.

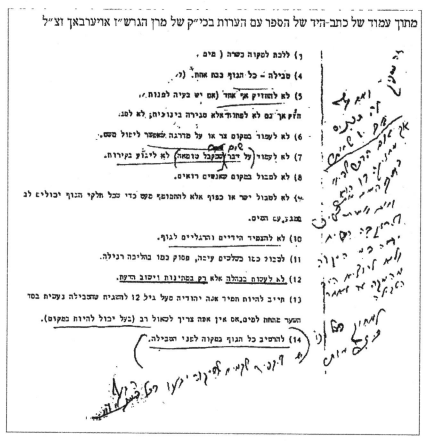

A manuscript page of *The Secret of Jewish Femininity,* with the handwritten emendations of HaRav Shlomo Zalman Auerbach, *zt"l*

בס"ד

המרכז הארצי למען טהרת המשפחה בישראל
ISRAEL CENTRAL COMMITTE FOR TAHARAS HAMISHPACHA

JERUSALEM, 18 YISAH BERACHA ST. P.O.B. 9067 .ר.ת 289414 .18 .טל ברכה ישא רח .ד.ת ירושלים

4 Adar Sheini, 5744

To the holy community, our brethren in Johannesburg, peace and all good things:

The value of the mitzvah of *taharas hamishpachah* is known to all. Our forefathers and foremothers made great sacrifices to observe the mitzvah in the proper time and to bequeath it to coming generations, for eternity. They knew that the Jewish family is a golden link in the chain of generations. Much to our distress, observance of this mitzvah has, of late, become weakened, and it now needs much strengthening and encouragement, and must be taught and explained.

Because the renowned activist Tehilla Abramov, *tichyeh*, is now among you — a most notable woman who works with us to counsel and teach the halachos of this mitzvah — we have asked her to take the opportunity during her stay in South Africa to found a women's organization whose task it is to strengthen the observance of *taharas hamishpachah*, and to increase the number of homes which will observe *taharas hamishpachah* and the sanctity of the home.

This organization will serve as the South African branch of our organization, both for teaching and for the distribution of explanatory materials, teaching and study materials, etc. Further elaboration of the subject is unnecessary, for every man and woman faithful to the nation of Israel and its Torah will correctly appreciate the great merit of those who assist in this lofty goal. May Hashem grant that you be among those who increase the number of Jewish families who will be a sanctuary for the Holy Presence, for many blessed generations.

Our blessing is that Hashem's kindness will be upon you, to grant you understanding and success in raising the purity of Israel and to merit, together with all of Israel, to speedily see the radiant face of *Mashiach Tzidkeinu*, Amen.

With blessings from the holy city, may it be rebuilt soon,

[signature]

Yehoshua Levi
The Israel Central Committee for Taharas HaMishpachah, Jerusalem

There is no need to add to the above. Fortunate is the man who is included in this great mitzvah — which is the basis for the survival of the purity and holiness of the House of Israel — and who brings greater purity to the establishment of kosher generations faithful to Hashem, and to His Torah and mitzvos.

[signature]

HaRav Shlomo Zalman Auerbach
President of the Israel Center for
Taharat Hamishpachah

[signature]

HaRav Sholom Mashash
Chief Rabbi, Jerusalem

ישיבת באר - יעקב
RABBINICAL COLLEGE YESHIVAT BE'ER-YAAKOV

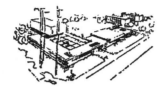

Joseph and Faye Tanenbaum
Education center

הרב מ. ש. שפירא
ראש הישיבה
RABBI M. S. SHAPIRO
Dean

BE'ER-YAAKOV ISRAEL
HAYESHIVA ST.

בס"ד. באר-יעקב.
רחוב הישיבה

(handwritten Hebrew letter)

10 Tevet, 5759

I declare the merit of Rebbetzin Tehilla Abramov, *tichyeh*, who is deserving of praise for her devoted work for *taharas hamishpachah*. She accomplishes much through her books, her appearances, and her lectures for the purity of Jewish women, with great knowledge. May G-d give her strength to accomplish and to help others accomplish in order to bring greater merit to the public.

With blessings,
Moshe Shmuel Shapiro

I hereby agree with the words above,
Yosef Sholom Elyashiv

8

RABBI S. WASSERMAN
PONIM MEIROT 15
MATERSDORF, JERUSALEM
ISRAEL

הרב שמחה וסרמן
רח' פנים מאירות 10/15
מטרסדורף - ירושלים

TEL. (02) 372 420 .טל

"And it shall come to pass that when all of these things which I have placed before you...the blessings and the curses...you will call them to mind...and you will return completely to Hashem...Hashem will also return to look after your exiles...and will have compassion on you..." (*Devarim* 30:1–3).

Our generation has witnessed the outpouring of the Divine wrath that caused unparalleled destruction and tragedy to our people. Now we are shown how the *hashgachah* rebuilds the Jewish nation by imbuing an ever-growing thirst for Torah and by inspiring the establishment of the happy and meaningful Jewish home. The *hashgachah*, at the same time, grants us its emissaries, to inspire the Jewish woman in her role as mother of a pure and holy generation, deserving to welcome Mashiach and our redemption.

I am grateful for the privilege of adding a note to this work which calls for the purity and holiness of the Jewish future.

Tishrei 5748

RABBI S. WASSERMAN
PONIM MEIROT 15
MATERSDORF, JERUSALEM
ISRAEL

TEL. (02) 372 420

הרב שמחה וסרמן
רח׳ פנים מאירות 15/10
מטרסדורף - ירושלים

טל.

Jerusalem, 12 Adar Alef, 5752

Well known is the esteemed Rebbetzin Tehilla Abramov, may she be blessed, who deals with encouraging and educating about the observance of holiness and *taharas hamishpachah* in Israel. Heaven has granted her great success in organizing groups of righteous women to observe and strengthen this mitzvah in many countries and Jewish communities. She has merited, also, to publish a book to encourage and teach the halachos of this mitzvah with the approval of the *gedolim* and *poskim* of our generation, HaGaon HaRav Shlomo Zalman Auerbach, *shlita* (*zt"l*), and HaGaon HaRav Yosef Sholom Elyashiv, *shlita*. The Rebbetzin is now planning to visit, with G-d's help, communities in the United States to publicize and strengthen this mitzvah, which all *Am Yisrael* depends upon. Surely the righteous everywhere will readily assist her for the sake of *kiddush shem Shamayim* and the holiness of *Am Yisrael* and its future.

Awaiting the speedy redemption and salvation of Israel.

Rabbi CHAIM P. SCHEINBERG
Rosh Hayeshiva "TORAH ORE"
and Morah Hora'ah of Kiryat Mattersdorf

הרב חיים פינחס שיינברג
ראש ישיבת "תורה אור"
ומורה הוראה דקרית מטרסדורף

Although I have not reviewed the halachos in this work, I deem it a privilege to write this letter of approbation for the idea behind it.

The survival of the Jewish people as a holy nation has always depended on the determination of its married women to live up to the Torah standards of *taharas hamishpachah* despite every obstacle. Legion are the tales of heroism displayed by daughters of Israel who braved the threats of enemies and dangers of climate to fulfill this special mitzvah, which endowed their families with purity and sanctity.

In our own time the physical obstacles are, thank G-d, no longer any impediment to a woman's ability to observe all the laws of family purity. The danger today is one of ignorance of the laws of *taharas hamishpachah* and the importance of observing them.

This is why it is such a pleasure to welcome the publication of an excellent work which presents both the laws and the significance of *taharas hamishpachah* in a style and language which so many of our generation so desperately require in order to become more familiar with a treasure which might otherwise remain beyond their reach. It is fitting that this work, the fruit of years of effort which Mrs. Tehilla Abramov has invested in promoting *taharas hamishpachah*, will, with G-d's help, be extended to the entire English-speaking world through the efforts of the Central Committee for Taharat HaMishpachah.

It is my *berachah* that Hashem bless with even greater success the historic efforts of all who disseminate the learning of *taharas hamishpachah* to our people and that Heaven open the eyes of all the daughters of Israel throughout the world to the treasure of personal and family happiness which awaits them when they live by the ideas presented in this work.

חיים פינחס שיינברג

Rabbi Chaim Pinchas Scheinberg
Tishrei 5748

Rabbi CHAIM P. SCHEINBERG
Rosh Hayeshiva "TORAH ORE"
and Morah Hora'ah of Kiryat Mattersdorf

הרב חיים פינחס שיינברג

ראש ישיבת "תורה אור"

ומורה הוראה דקרית מטרסדורף

1 Sivan 5762

The esteemed Rabbi Yirmiyohu Abramov, *shlita*, and his wife, *tichyeh*, are already renowned for their lofty efforts, done with the greatest dedication and without any financial remuneration, solely to assist *Klal Yisrael* in acquiring the *Toras HaBayis* in halachah and *hashkafah* which constitutes the sanctity of the Jewish people.

As has been stated in the past, all the halachos [in the book] were examined in great detail by the great men, the luminaries of the generation, as well as the methods of teaching the topic and the training of counselors, in order to strengthen Jewish souls in their observance of G-d's mitzvos.

As is well known, diligent scholars accompany them, and every detail is carried out in accordance with their dictates.

Many homes in Israel and all over the world have been established on foundations of holiness thanks to their guidance. Through their direct influence and the influence of their counselors they have succeeded in rescuing many homes from the "destruction" of which it says, "even the altar sheds tears" [i.e., divorce].

As "Only the diligent deserve encouragement," I recommend that they be encouraged and their work strengthened, so that they can continue in their extraordinary and tireless endeavors.

And may Hashem's Grace rest upon them.

בס"ד

עובדיה יוסף
הראשון לציון, נשיא מועצת חכמי התורה

[handwritten letter in Hebrew]

To the well-known Rebbetzin, an activist for Torah, Mrs. Tehilla Abramov, may she be blessed:

I was delighted to hear of the publication of the book *The Secret of Jewish Femininity: Insights into the Practice of Taharat HaMishpachah*, which was beautifully written by you in consultation with outstanding rabbinic authorities, who carefully went over all the laws in the book and gave their approval to their delineation.

I am certain this book will help bring many Jewish women closer to their origins, to keep *taharat hamishpachah* properly in accordance with its laws, and to understand the importance of purity.

In view of the importance of the laws pertaining to these matters, and in view of the differences between the customs and laws of the Sephardim and Edot HaMizrach, and the Ashkenazim, I have asked my son, Rabbi David Yosef, *shlita*, to carefully review the sections of laws in the book, and to point out the differences in customs and laws between the various groups. His comments, based on my instructions, are included as an appendix at the end of the book.

I give my blessing that you be able to make a blessing on the completion [of the book]. May G-d grant you success in giving over your wellsprings so that you bring the hearts of the daughters of Israel to the understanding of the value of *taharat hamishpachah*, and to increase Torah and glorify it.

With honor and Torah blessings,   **Ovadia Yosef**

משה הלברשטאם
מו"צ העדה החרדית
ראש ישיבת "דברי חיים" טשאקאווע
מח"ס שו"ת "דברי משה"
פעיה"ק ירושלים תובב"א
רח' יואל 8 טל. 372514

20 Menachem Av 5756 BS"D

Well known is the preciousness of the holiness of the Jewish home, as well as the value of peace between man and wife; so much so that the Sages declare: "Hashem says: Let My Name be erased in order to bring peace between man and his wife."

As I know very well, in spite of the high and lofty value of the holiness of the home, there are still many Jewish homes in which peace and harmony do not dwell. The Rabbis see with sorrowful hearts the harsh results of a lack of suitable guidance and instruction to ensure the building and maintaining of a kosher and faithful Jewish home.

Let us now show our gratitude to those who have lately started a worthwhile activity: to organize courses — taught by experienced rebbetzins — to train counselors who will be prepared to teach the observant daughters of Israel here in the Holy City of Jerusalem, and give them appropriate instruction, both in the relevant halachos and in the correct way to maintain a home and build it according to our holy Torah, on the solid foundation of holiness and purity, peace, love, friendship, and goodwill.

As this matter has been carried out in conjunction with the important organization Jewish Marriage Education, which was founded by the outstanding *mezakeh harabim* Rabbi Yirmiyohu Abramov, *shlita*, and his wife, the Rebbetzin, *tichyeh*, who have spent many years dealing with these matters in Israel and abroad, under the direction of *gedolei Yisrael, shlita*; and we have already heard and seen that they have merited special Heavenly assistance and great success; I therefore extend my hand to them and their endeavors and say to them, *Yasher Koach*.

Undoubtedly, it is very important that every virtuous daughter of Israel receive proper guidance, both before and after her marriage, to build her home on a solid foundation of peace and harmony, in accordance with the desire of our Creator, blessed be His Name.

May Hashem bless you and your Rebbetzin in your activities of increasing peace, love, and friendship. May Hashem spread His peace on us and on all Israel and on Jerusalem, may it be speedily rebuilt in our day, Amen.

Moshe Halberstam

יצחק זילברשטיין
רב שכונת רמת אלחנן
בני ברק

כ"ג מרחשון תש[illegible]

כדי שהספרים סוד הנגלה והגלוי, "ונעים שמם אחד"
שחיברו הרה"ג הרבנים אברהם שליט"א, יהיו שוים לכל,
גם לבנות ישראל, חכמים הסומכים [illegible], בקשני
מו"ח גאון ישראל מרן רבי יוסף שלום אלישיב שליט"א לעיין ולומר
על הספרים הנ"ל, ופקדתו שמרה נפשי, והשמטתי
והכנסתי בהם דברים, והיינו בעזר אחי עם הרבנים הגאונים
ר' שמחה הכהן קוק שליט"א ור' אריה דביר שליט"א
ובאמת שהספרים ראוים להעלות על שלחן בנות מלכים הנבחרות ולנשים
מלכה, ואני מקוה להשיג שהספרים יביאו תועלת לבנות ישראל שיגנו
בתורה בקדושה ובטהרה על דרך הסלולה לנו מאבותינו ואמותינו
הקדושים. ועל באתי על החתום. יצחק זילברשטיין

יצחק זילברשטיין רב שכונת רמת אלחנן בני ברק ת"א

שמחה הכהן קוק

אריה דביר

מרן הגאון הרב יוסף שלום אלישיב שליט"א:

[illegible]

מרן הגאון הרב משה שמואל שפירא שליט"א:

בס"ד.
דברי הרבנים הגאונים שליט"א [illegible]
[illegible]
[illegible]
[illegible]
[illegible]
[illegible]

RABBI YITCHAK SILBERSTEIN　　יצחק זילברשטיין
Rabbi of Ramat Elchanan　　רב שכונת רמת אלחנן
BNEI-BRAK　　בני–ברק

16 Marcheshvan 5763

In order that the books *The Secret of Jewish Femininity* and *Two Halves of a Whole*, written by Rabbi and Rebbetzin Abramov, *shlita*, be suitable to all, including *bnos Yisrael* educated in Bais Yaakov, I was asked by my teacher, my father-in-law, the *gaon* of Israel, Maran HaRav Yosef Sholom Elyashiv, *shlita*, to read and review these books, and I obeyed his instructions.

In consultation with the rabbanim, the *gaonim* Rav Simcha HaCohen Kook, *shlita*, and Rav Aryeh Dvir, *shlita*, I added and deleted certain items, and I feel the books are worthy of being placed on the table of the daughters of kings, and can be used to lecture from.

We hope to *Hashem Yisbarach* that the books will bring benefit to the daughters of Israel and that they will build their homes in holiness and purity, following the road paved by our holy forefathers and foremothers.

Upon this we sign,

Yitzchak Zilberstein

Simcha Kook

Aryeh Dvir

I hereby add my blessing to the Abramov family, that they succeed in their important work, in consultation and with the guidance of these above-mentioned great rabbanim.

Yosef Sholom Elyashiv

With G-d's help:

There is no need to reaffirm the words of the great rabbis, *shlita*. May the blessings of Hashem rest upon the works of the *mezakei harabim*, dear people who have put great efforts into increasing the purity within Israel under the guidance of *gedolei Torah*, Rabbi and Rebbetzin Abramov, and may they continue their important endeavor, under the guidance of the *gedolei Torah*, *shlita*, for many more years.

With blessings,

Moshe Shmuel Shapiro

16

Rabbi Yisroel Gans	הרב ישראל גנס
2 Panim Meirot	רח' פנים מאירות 2
Kiryat Mattersdorf, Jerusalem	קרית מטרסדורף, ירושלים

I have seen the book *The Secret of Jewish Femininity*, written by Mrs. Tehilla Abramov, *tichyeh*, and reviewed the halachic portion of it, and have found the book worthy of publication. It serves an important purpose for women, and learning it will undoubtedly increase the purity of Israel.

May it be His will that in the merit of this great mitzvah *HaKadosh Baruch Hu* will place upon us the spirit of purity from On High, and we will merit the final redemption and the coming of *Mashiach Tzidkeinu* speedily, in our days, Amen.

Tishrei 5748

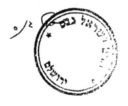

RABBI J. ROTH
1556 - 53rd Street
Brookly, N.Y. 11219
Tel. (718) 435-1502

יחזקאל ראטה
אבדק"ק קארלסבורג
בארא פארק, ברוקלין, נ.י. יע"א

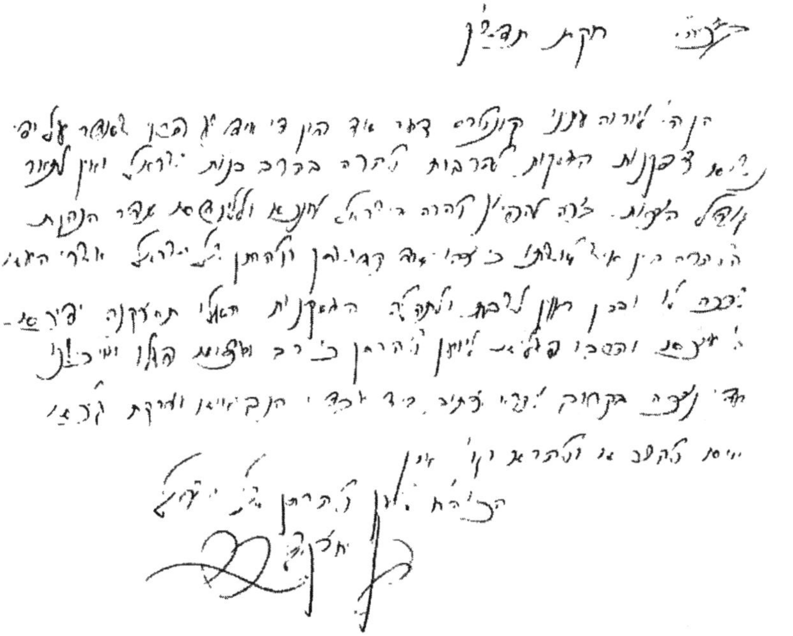

B"SD, Chukas 5750

The book *The Secret of Jewish Femininity*, that was put together by righteous women who work to increase purity among the daughters of Israel, was brought before me. There is no way to describe the great merit of spreading this purity throughout Israel, to instruct and to teach the purity of behavior between a man and his wife: this is the secret of the holiness and purity of Israel, and fortunate is the nation for whom this is so. Therefore these activists are worthy of acclaim and praise. May their hands be strengthened; may Hashem be with them; and may they increase their activities on behalf of purity, for their deeds are great and who can enumerate them? May we soon merit to see the words of the prophet: "And I shall throw pure water upon you, and you will be pure..." Amen.

Signed for the sake of the purity of Israel,

Yechezkel Roth

18

Menachem Mendel Weissmandel   מנחם מאיר וייסמאנדל

Av Beis Din Kahal Toras Chamad D'Nitra   אב״ד קהל תורת חמ״ד דנייטרא

Monsey, New York   מאנסי נ.י.

It is a pleasure for me to testify about something that I am personally familiar with: the numerous activities of the women who teach the laws of purity to the daughters of Israel, in purity and holiness, with sacrifice, dedication and scrupulous accuracy. They patiently teach the practical halachos to every individual privately, in a way that ensures they make no mistakes and will know how to observe *taharas hamishpachah* and the holiness of a daughter of Israel. More, they have taught the daughters of Israel the outlook of the Torah and of our traditions on matters of extreme importance, in accordance with the abilities of each to accept it, in order to bring greater holiness and to increase modesty, so as to create generations faithful to Hashem and His Torah, in the spirit of the Sages, and with the encouragement and counsel of the great men, the lights of Israel, *shlita*. All this was under the guidance of, and organized by, a woman of wisdom, a woman who does great things and fears G-d, Mrs. Abramov, may she live long.

Her book, *The Secret of Jewish Femininity* has now been published in Yiddish. [The readers] may review important things within it, things which, Heaven fordbid, might be forgotten. I was shown the portion dealing with the halachos, in order to give my approbation. They were given over properly, in accordance with the law, in the way it is proper to teach daughters of Israel, with methodology accepted by the greatest of our teachers.

May it be His will that they continue to increase Torah and glorify it.

9 Nisan, 5755

Monsey

OHR SOMAYACH אור שמח

Each generation, say our Talmudic Sages, has its own special needs, its own unique form of communication, and its own Heaven-sent individuals to effectively communicate the answers to its needs.

In an age when the sacred institution of marriage is so threatened by the excesses of a permissive and self-centered society, many Jews have begun to look to the time-honored practice of Family Purity as an anchor for the preservation of their personal identity and their marital happiness.

Rather than looming as a final destination on the road of commitment to a Torah lifestyle, Family Purity has emerged as a major catalyst in convincing the newcomer of the tangible benefits of living in harmony with the prescription offered by the divine Creator of man and woman.

This exciting potential of courses in Jewish Marriage Education was discovered by Mrs. Tehilla Abramov, wife of Ohr Somayach educational director, Rabbi Yirmiyohu Abramov, while assisting her husband a few years ago during his tour of duty as the head of Ohr Somayach operations in the Jewish community of South Africa. The scores of families who went from these courses on Jewish marriage to a fuller experiencing of a Torah life inspired her to extend these efforts upon returning to Israel. In addition to her work with the Central Committee for Taharat HaMishpachah as a trainer of Family Purity counselors, she also gives a course for the wives of the participants in the Ohr Somayach Teachers Training Program committed to assisting their husbands in communicating Jewish values throughout the world.

This book is both the echo of the historic work which Mrs. Abramov and her colleagues have done on several continents, and a harbinger of the dramatic impact which education in Family Purity is certain to have on an entire generation anxious to discover the wisdom and beauty of a Torah-guided life, and to strengthen themselves in the observance of its requirements.

The entire Jewish community salutes the Central Committee for Taharat HaMishpachah and Mrs. Abramov upon this publication of a truly effective response to the most sensitive need of our generation.

Mendel Weinbach

Rabbi Mendel Weinbach
Dean, Ohr Somayach Institutions

20

המרכז הארצי למען טהרת המשפחה בישראל
ISRAEL CENTRAL COMMITTE FOR TAHARAS HAMISHPACHA

JERUSALEM, 18 YISAH BERACHA ST. P.O.B. 5067, ירושלים ת"ד, רח' ישא ברכה 18. טל. 285414. ת.ד.

This book is based on a manual for *Taharat HaMishpachah* teachers written in Hebrew by Mrs. Tehilla Abramov, which was published by our organization. We are proud and delighted to be part of this unique presentation to the English public, who will surely find much of interest in it.

The material printed was prepared in consultation with *gedolei hador:* our president, HaGaon Rav Shlomo Zalman Auerbach, *shlita,* and in certain matters, with HaGaon Rav Sholom Yosef Elyashiv, *shlita.*

We have published many booklets on the subject of *Taharat HaMishpachah,* some of which have been printed in twelve languages and published in hundreds of thousands of copies.

Our monumental organization is the only one of its kind in Eretz Yisrael, and we specifically apply ourselves to the building and renovating of *mikvaot* in small settlements in cooperation and coordination with the government, for example the Ministry for Religious Affairs and local municipalities.

In addition, we have a special technical department (similar to a First Aid Department) for the daily repairing of *mikvaot.*

In addition to our written publications, we have a department for teaching and counseling which is staffed by hundreds of teachers and counselors who make home visits, give classes and lectures, etc.

The existence of our organization is dependent solely on the generosity of fellow Jews throughout the world.

With multiple blessings from the Holy City of Jerusalem,

HaRav Yehoshua Levy
Director

My thanks to —

Mrs. Malka Touger, whose creative writing skills have enabled this book to emerge form my original Hebrew *Taharat HaMishpachah* teachers' manual and lecture tapes into its present form.

The staff at Targum Press for their devoted efforts in the publishing of this book.

All those whose encouragement was the force which made this book a reality.

This book is dedicated to —

All the wonderful women in Eretz Yisrael and abroad whose authentic experiences appear in this book and which serve as an inspiration to us all in the observance of *Taharat HaMishpachah*. (For obvious reasons, names and places have all been changed.)

All the *Taharat HaMishpachah* teachers and counselors worldwide, whose sincere efforts have affected the lives of so many.

Although the halachot in this book have been thoroughly checked by Rabbinical authorities, it is my fervent request that they be studied together with a *Taharat HaMishpachah* counselor in order that all the details be fully understood.

May we merit that all Jewish homes be built in holiness and purity and that peace should reign therein.

And may we merit the complete redemption with the coming of *Mashiach Tzidkeinu* speedily in our days.

With heartfelt praise and gratitude to *Hashem Yisbarach,*

Tehilla Abramov

In memory of our dear parents
לעילוי נשמות הורינו היקרים

My mother, my teacher	My father, my teacher
מרת חסיה ב״ר אברהם איסר	ר׳ אוריאל חיים ב״ר ישראל
אברמוב ע״ה	**אברמוב** ז״ל
נלב״ע ב׳ בתשרי תשנ״ב	נלב״ע ב׳ בניסן תשכ״ד
ת.נ.צ.ב.ה.	ת.נ.צ.ב.ה.

My mother, my teacher	My father, my teacher
מרת רבקה ב״ר שלום	ר׳ ישראל אלכסנדר ב״ר חיים בן-ציון
כץ ע״ה	**כץ** ז״ל
נלב״ע ז׳ במנחם אב תש״ס	נלב״ע ט״ו באדר תשמ״ה
ת.נ.צ.ב.ה.	ת.נ.צ.ב.ה.

In memory of our dear grandparents
לעילוי נשמות זקנינו היקרים

ר׳ אברהם איסר ב״ר דוד שלמה	ר׳ ישראל ב״ר אברהם
שלומוביץ ז״ל	**אברמוב** ז״ל
נלב״ע ה׳ באדר ראשון תש״ו	נלב״ע כ״ח באדר תרצ״ז
ת.נ.צ.ב.ה.	ת.נ.צ.ב.ה.

מרת שרה ב״ר משה	מרת דבורה ב״ר שלמה
שלומוביץ ע״ה	**אברמוב** ע״ה
נלב״ע א׳ במנחם אב תשי״ב	נלב״ע י׳ בתשרי תשי״ד
ת.נ.צ.ב.ה.	ת.נ.צ.ב.ה.

ר׳ שלום ב״ר צבי	ר׳ חיים בן-ציון ב״ר שלום
אסטרוף ז״ל	**כץ** הי״ד
נלב״ע כ״ג בשבט תש״ז	נלב״ע בחורבן אירופה
ת.נ.צ.ב.ה.	ת.נ.צ.ב.ה.

מרת רחל פרידא ב״ר אבא נתן	מרת רחל גליקא ב״ר שמואל
אוסטרוף ע״ה	**כץ** הי״ד
נלב״ע כ״ח בניסן תשל״ח	נלב״ע בחורבן אירופה
ת.נ.צ.ב.ה.	ת.נ.צ.ב.ה.

In memory of our dear teacher

לעילוי נשמת רבנו מורה דרכנו

מרן הגאון

רבי שלמה זלמן אויערבאך זצוק"ל

נלב"ע כ' באדר ראשון תשנ"ה

ת.נ.צ.ב.ה.

In memory of our dear teacher

לעילוי נשמת רבנו מורה דרכנו

מרן הגאון

רבי יוסף שלום אלישיב זצוק"ל

נלב"ע כ"ח בתמוז תשע"ב

ת.נ.צ.ב.ה.

Contents

Chapter 1

The Secret of Jewish Femininity

SHIMON'S GOOD FORTUNE had brought him through the open door of one of the Warsaw Jewish community's wealthiest, most generous households. Every evening, the family and the many poor wayfarers invited as guests would gather together for a sumptuous dinner.

Shimon's mouth watered at the thought that he would be able to partake of this feast. He had been away from home for weeks, and many days had passed since he had enjoyed a full meal. As he looked around the table, his eyes widened at the exquisite furnishings and the elegance.

Finally, it was time for the meal. The head of the house rose from his place, removed a small crystal bell from his pocket, and sounded it once. Servants quickly appeared carrying trays laden with food. They graciously served all those assembled and returned to the kitchen.

When the first course was completed, the host again rang the bell. Servants reappeared, cleared off the tables, and returned shortly afterward with the second course. The same pattern was repeated each time. The host would ring the bell and, in response, servants would bring another course of delicacies.

Shimon barely had time to savor the last bite of the delicious dessert when his host astounded all the guests by informing them that each one could take with him a gift. "You may choose anything you desire — one of the silver spoons, the crystal goblets, whatever you fancy," he announced.

Shimon did not hesitate. One item alone had captured his attention. "If only I had a bell like that, I would never want for food," he thought. When Shimon made his request, his host stared in disbelief. "Are you sure? There are much more valuable things in this house. Take a crystal goblet, a piece of silver. Why would you want the bell?" he asked.

But Shimon couldn't be swayed. When he repeated his request, his host granted him his wish. Thanking him for his generosity, Shimon placed the bell in his pocket and began his journey home. All along the way, he congratulated himself on his wise choice. "Never another worry about our next meal," he thought to himself.

Shimon's wife had been anticipating his return. She had run out of supplies, and their creditors were hounding her to pay their long-overdue accounts. Shimon, she hoped, would be returning with both money and supplies after having conducted business in the city.

When his wife sighted his approaching figure, she took heart at the obviously content look on her husband's face. "Shimon, what have you brought home?" she asked impatiently after they had greeted each other.

"Don't worry, dear wife," he assured her. "This was a very successful trip. We'll never have to worry again. But I'll explain everything after dinner."

"What dinner!" his wife cried in dismay. "Whatever supplies you left ran out weeks ago. You didn't leave any money either.

How am I supposed to make you dinner?"

He confidently beckoned his wife to join him at the table. With a serious and dignified look on his face, he rose, reached into his pocket, took out his crystal bell, and rang it gently.

His wife looked on in disbelief. Why would her husband ring the bell and then turn to the kitchen in anticipation? "What on earth is this all about?" she burst out in frustration.

Shimon only shook his head in disappointment. "I don't understand," he mumbled to himself again and again. "It worked so well in the rich man's house..."

(Dubno Maggid)

All of us occasionally make Shimon's mistake of thinking we can have that which we desire without working for it. Recognizing this truth, that nothing worthwhile comes without effort, may make all the difference between a successful or failed marriage.

It is known that a woman's fundamental hope in life is that she will have a husband...

(The Steipler)

Naturally the husband she hopes for is one who respects her and cares for her. Indeed there isn't a girl who doesn't grow up with thoughts of a happy marriage. Every woman by nature looks forward to finding a man after her own heart with whom to build a joint life. She follows the prescribed path to marriage but often without too much thought about the deeper significance of what she is doing. Consequently, and sometimes only a few short months after the marriage, she wakes up and realizes that for a marriage to be meaningful and satisfying — for a marriage to work — "bell ringing" is not enough. Marriage is more than a ceremony. The glamour and glitter of the wedding soon become pictures in an album, and a woman confronts the need to relate beyond herself and give genuine happiness to a husband and a family. It is not long before the starry-eyed and blissful bride is jolted into the realization that for her marriage to grow into a success she must find a standard of values which will help her to understand what it means to be a woman, guide her in developing realistic expectations of married life, and make her aware of the depth of commitment she must make to marriage and family in order for them to work.

The story of the feminist movement, widespread in this generation, is the story of women's struggle to orient themselves within the framework of modern society.

They declare, "We're dissatisfied with the role society has mapped out for us, and we want to arrive at a new definition." However, after years of grappling with the issue, contemporary feminism has not offered a viable system of values. In fact, despite the women's serious struggle, morality has declined. The very institution of marriage is being questioned, the birthrate has plummeted, and women continue to feel that society is using and abusing them.

A PEDIATRICIAN WHO accepted Torah practice after having been raised in a secular home disclosed to a friend, "I was religious for two years before I really believed in G-d."

Her listener was amazed: "How could you follow Torah laws if you didn't have that basic commitment?"

"I looked at families with Torah homes, and I saw their lifestyle. I was impressed with the women and felt they were more in touch with themselves than my contemporaries. Marriage wasn't a burden to them, but an expression of who they were. I became convinced that the excellent communication between husbands and wives and parents and children was a result of their Jewish

practice. I wanted a home where these values could be realized. I wasn't going to allow my belief or lack of it to stand in the way."

The Torah system of values has produced families regarded as the epitome of stability and happiness for thousands of years. This has proven to be true whatever the society, whatever the culture Jews have found themselves a part of.

At no time has the contrast between the values Judaism stresses and those of the society around it been more pronounced than today. A look at the reasons for the skyrocketing divorce rate tells part of the story.

Dr. Domeena Renshaw, of Chicago's Loyola University, states that 80 percent of the divorces in Western society come about because of incompatibility within the couples' private lives. Furthermore, 50 percent of the couples who remain married have problems in this area.

Even without these statistics we can get an idea of the problem. The proliferation of clinics, specialists, manuals, and counselors, all offering the "secret" to problem-free relations, attests to the difficulty modern society has in finding the proper balance between husband and wife.

These difficulties stem from the secular world's approach, which stresses and recognizes only physicality and bodily pleasures — a physical perspective that undermines and degrades women. In contrast, Judaism recognizes a spiritual reality to which a Jewish woman can contribute.

When we proclaim "Hear Israel, G-d is our Lord, G-d is One," we are not merely negating the existence of a second divinity; we are emphasizing how His transcendent Oneness pervades and permeates every aspect of the Creation. If this is true regarding the world at large, it must surely apply to the union between man and woman.

> *Know that the act of union is a holy and pure matter when carried out in the proper manner, at the proper time, and with the proper intentions. A person should not think there is anything degrading or unbecoming in the act of union, G-d forbid.*
>
> (Ramban, Iggeret HaKodesh, ch. 2)

Moreover, we see that the *Zohar* describes the union of a couple in marriage as the coming together of two half-souls. The union completes the expression of their total bond and, consequently, must be viewed as a G-dly experience.

Such a perspective adds a new dimension to the woman's role. She is an equal partner in this holy activity. Her union with her husband is an opportunity for bringing another aspect of G-d's Oneness into the world.

> *And he shall cling to his wife and they shall become one flesh.*
>
> (Bereishit 2:24)

The numerical value of the Hebrew word for one, *echad*, is thirteen. When two "ones" get married, their two numerical values are added together and the sum is twenty-six. This is the numerical equivalent of G-d's name. Again, we see that, in Jewish thought, when a couple join together in a genuine bond, they reflect and reveal G-d's Presence.

> *She should also join with him in holy and refined thoughts. Then, their minds will be fused as one...and they will both be united at this time, and G-d's Presence will rest between them.*
>
> (Ramban, Iggeret HaKodesh, ch. 5)

The idea that there is holiness in married life is something intuitively understandable to a woman. In the morning, men recite the blessing *shelo asani ishah*, thanking G-d for "not making me a woman." However, women praise Him with the blessing *she'asani kirtzono*, for "making me according to His will." The commentaries explain that men recite this blessing in appreciation for the opportunity they have been given to fulfill more mitzvot. The Kabbalists add that the fact that women do not ask for the opportunity to perform more mitzvot is a reflection of their unique nature.

What is the intent of the mitzvot? To train our human natures to be attuned to G-d's will. Men are given more mitzvot because they require more training. Women by nature do not require as much "training," because they possess a natural, intuitive connection to G-d's will.

Surely, woman's clearer understanding of G-d's will allows her to understand and feel holiness and spirituality in all areas of life, including married life. Therefore, the merely physical aspects of marriage are often not sufficient for her. She strives for spirituality, and many times even more so than her husband.

> *...And thy desire shall be to thy husband and he shall rule over thee.*
>
> *(Bereishit 3:16)*

All four times that the word *teshukah*, "desire," appears in the Torah it refers to spiritual desire. Therefore, it can be explained that Rashi in his explanation on this verse is referring to spiritual desire. G-d put into the nature of the woman the natural inclination to recognize the true essence of married life in both its physical and spiritual aspects.

The Torah calls the commandment of marital intimacy "*onah*," similar to the word *la'anot* — to respond. The husband is obligated to "respond" to her needs, implying that a man must attune himself to his wife and her desire for holiness and spirituality in the marriage.

The holiness and spirituality which are the cornerstone of marriage require clear guidelines from the source of holiness and spirituality; that is, the Creator. These guidelines are the laws of *Taharat HaMishpachah*, which follow a woman's own natural rhythms and inclinations and give expression to her desire for privacy and individuality on one hand and closeness coupled with respect and appreciation on the other.

Taharat HaMishpachah is the secret of Jewish femininity. It provides the couple with a divinely ordained framework of commandments showing them how to relate to each other and express and build their happiness and devotion. On this sturdy foundation, they can construct a superstructure of family and home. The study of these ideas and their application within the context of our lives will help each of us discover insights which are ancient, for they were given by G-d on Mount Sinai, but at the same time contemporary, for they are continually relevant to our lives as women and as Jews.

Women have the ability and willingness to search for spirituality in their marriage and to tirelessly dedicate themselves to the furtherance of this spiritual growth. A beautiful example of this is Devorah, the wife of Lapidot, who raised her husband's spiritual level by providing him with wicks for the Tabernacle, thus ensuring he would be in the company of righteous men. (She was rewarded for her actions as we know: she became Devorah the prophetess.) Through their fervent prayers, too, women help elevate themselves and their spouses. This, too, is the secret of Jewish femininity.

Chapter 2

The Changing Status

DAVID, 24, AND DALYA, 21, *had known each other for some time when they decided to get married. The couple set a date for their wedding in eight weeks. As their families wanted a traditional ceremony, David and Dalya chose an Orthodox rabbi to officiate. But, as the two now freely admit, the choice of rabbi really made no difference to them, since neither was religious. With casual indifference, they arrived at the Rabbi's house for an appointment. The Rabbi greeted them warmly and invited them into his study.*

"Congratulations on your engagement," he smiled at the couple. "I'd be pleased to officiate at your wedding. But, I want you to understand that a Jewish marriage is not a casual matter. There's a lot involved..."

"He's trying to explain why he is going to ask for a high fee," David mused to himself. "It's okay, Rabbi," he cut him off. "You don't have to worry about the fee."

"No, I'm not talking about my fee or even the ceremony itself. In Judaism, a marriage is more than standing together under the marriage canopy. I invited you over to share some thoughts and

insights on the way Judaism looks at marriage."

"Oh, no!" groaned David to himself, as the Rabbi paused for a moment. "I bet we're in for a sermon..."

"I thought we were just going to finalize details," thought Dalya. "Now, we have to sit through a lecture..."

They gave each other a glance of mutual resolve: They would endure this ordeal with respect and understanding. This would be their first and last visit to the Rabbi.

"You must both be very preoccupied with wedding preparations," the Rabbi said. "I appreciate your coming despite your busy schedules. You see, we too often concern ourselves solely with wedding preparations while overlooking the need to prepare for the marriage itself.

"The books on those shelves," the Rabbi continued, pointing to several large volumes, "talk about family life in general and about married life in particular, and not only about the ceremony."

The Rabbi continued: "I believe my wife would be better able to explain the details to you, Dalya, than I would." He gestured toward a smartly dressed woman who had been busy in the adjoining room.

Dalya sighed, "I hope I'm not going to get a quick course on preparing gefilte fish and matzo balls from the 'Rebbetzin'!" Reluctantly, she joined the rabbi's wife in the living room.

In fact, their conversation involved far more than simply a cooking lesson. For the first time in her life, Dalya heard an Orthodox Jewish woman talk openly about Jewish married life in all its aspects. Dalya was amazed at the familiarity and ease with which the Rebbetzin discussed matters which she thought were taboo and improper for observant people.

"You mean all this is actually mentioned in the Bible?" she asked in surprise.

"Of course!" came the reply. "G-d created our bodies. He put the capacity to give happiness in our hearts. Isn't it logical to assume that He also wanted to teach man (and woman!) how and to whom to give happiness?"

That first chat turned out to be just the beginning. What was meant to be a one-time encounter turned into a series of sessions spent with the Rabbi and his wife learning the subject of Taharat HaMishpachah. Abstention from physical contact between husband and wife during menstruation and for the seven days following, and immersion in the mikveh, were presented not only as a G-dly command, but also as a practice leading to personal growth and marital happiness.

David's parents were divorced. He deeply wanted his marriage to succeed and soon realized that the ideas being presented to him anticipated and answered his concerns. The Torah's approach to marriage convinced him of the need to study and discover more of what Judaism had to offer.

Dalya sensed a new dimension in her anticipation of their upcoming wedding. She began to feel that a Torah lifestyle would enhance her ability to express her happiness, whereas the values modern society held out as the ideal for women ignored this aspect of her personality. David and Dalya decided to take on the challenge.

Looking back, David remembers that hard beginning with a chuckle. "We agreed to bear with separation till the wedding. Whenever I showed signs of weakness it was Dalya who put me straight, and the time till the wedding went by with excitement and anticipation."

The highlight of this new experience was Dalya's immersion in the mikveh. "I can't describe the feeling. All I can say is that it made it all very, very special." Dalya's going to the mikveh was not a one-time affair. She is delighted to be able to recapture the feeling, for both she and David have committed themselves to keeping a Jewish home.

"At first, David was hesitant. He didn't really believe we could do it. But now, well, it's grown on us, and we've grown through it. I look at some of my friends, who are still searching for a deeper sense of meaning in their relationships with their husbands, and say to myself, 'There, but for the grace of G-d (and the Rabbi's wife!) go I.' "

Dalya and David were granted Heavenly assistance. They recognized that the marriage bonds between a man and his wife present an opportunity to introduce an added measure of holiness into one's life, even into that area which is most intimate. This additional holiness immeasurably strengthens the relationship between a man and his wife.

A line connecting two points is easily broken, whereas a triangle is the sturdiest geometric form. Similarly, a marriage must be more than a bond between man and woman. We need a third partner — G-d. The Master of the universe, the Creator of all beings, designed a unique plan for achieving the maximum fulfillment that marriage can offer. The laws of *Taharat HaMishpachah* provide the framework for this plan.

The laws of *Taharat HaMishpachah* revolve around the intimate relationship between man and wife. A man and a woman make a mutual commitment to fulfill these commandments — to express their affection for one another within the rhythms of the woman's physical cycle. During the days of the month when a woman has her menstrual period, she is considered a *niddah*. The root of this Hebrew word is *nadad* — to separate. While a *niddah*, a woman separates from her husband. As her physical state changes, she prepares herself emotionally and spiritually for the time when she and her husband will be together again. After immersion in a *mikveh*, the couple are reunited in a spirit of holiness and purity.

The observance of the laws of *Taharat HaMishpachah* strengthens every Jewish marriage. Moreover, the care with which they have been followed has been one of the major factors ensuring the survival of our people. The faithful practice of these laws throughout the generations has added link after link in Judaism's golden chain.

We inherited the commitment to keep these laws, even under the most trying circumstances, from our ancestors in ancient Egypt. Enslaved and compelled to perform hard labor, the men's spirits soon faltered. They no longer desired marital relations. They could not bear to see the children they conceived flung into the roaring waters of the Nile river. In desperation, they avoided their wives, unwilling to bring further sorrow upon their families.

It was the women who were filled with hope and belief. Their inner strength inspired them to seek out their husbands and encourage them to father a next generation regardless of their present hardships. These women observed the laws of Family Purity in the depths of slavery, determined that the Jewish nation would carry on.

When the women prepared to be with their husbands, they took great pains to appear attractive. Lacking even the most basic cosmetic tools, they used copper plaques for mirrors. With prayers in their hearts, they scrubbed the copper till it shone in order that they could see their reflections.

> *In the merit of the righteous women, Israel were redeemed from Egypt.*
>
> *(Sotah 11b)*

Our Sages declared that the Jewish people were redeemed from Egypt in the merit of those righteous women. It was because the women recognized the holiness inherent in marital relations and family life in general that they were able to persevere and raise a new generation that would emerge a new nation: the Jewish people.

Their commitment was not forgotten. At the giving of the Torah on Mount Sinai, G-d commanded the Jewish people to build a Tabernacle. Every individual was anxious to contribute to the fashioning of this holy structure. In addition to gifts of gold and silver, the women donated their prized personal possessions: those handmade copper mirrors.

Moshe Rabbeinu was reluctant to accept such a contribution. He questioned the mirrors' apparent lack of holiness and refinement. Their purpose was so clearly physically oriented. Noticing his indecision, G-d revealed Himself to Moshe: "Take them. They're dearer to Me than anything else." G-d instructed Moshe to melt the copper plaques and construct the basin used in the Tabernacle from that very metal. Before the priests began their service in the Tabernacle, they would wash from this basin, reminding themselves of the unique dedication of the Jewish women, for it was they who understood that holiness in religious life cannot be separated from holiness in family life (*Rashi, Shemot 38:8*).

> *Every practice for which Israel has sacrificed itself has been maintained.*
>
> (*Mechilta, Ki Tisah*)

There are no other mitzvot that have proven such a challenge to women as those surrounding the observance of *Taharat HaMishpachah*. The determination of our foremothers in Egypt is but one example. Throughout the generations, Jewish women have provided us with a legacy of strength and courage in their observance of the laws of *Taharat HaMishpachah*. Recent archaeological discoveries at Masada, for instance, indicate that the Jewish defenders of that clifftop site maintained an extensive system of *mikvaot*. Even in the midst of a life-and-death struggle, they never lost sight of exactly what they were fighting for.

Masada
(from the book Mikvaot *by architect Yosef Sheinberger,*
reprinted with permission)

But we needn't even go back that far to find examples of brave determination to follow G-d's will...

"YOU ASK WHY I AM CRYING?" exclaims a newly arrived immigrant from behind the Iron Curtain. Seated in the comfortable waiting room of an attractive mikveh building in Eretz Yisrael, Mrs. Krovsky wipes a tear from her eye as she relates her experiences to the mikveh attendant.

"It's less than a month since we left Russia. This is the first

time I'm going to the mikveh without worrying who is looking over my shoulder.

"There are hundreds of women in Russia who keep Taharat HaMishpachah. It is extremely difficult, especially if you have young children and you work outside your home. My sixteen years of married life were a story of hiding, secrecy, and fear. Going to a mikveh was always a logistical nightmare. Where to go? How to get there? How to avoid suspicion? How to meet the travel expenses?

"You can't imagine the commitment marriage demands from an observant Jew in Russia. While most brides were concerned with wedding preparations, I was preoccupied with constructing a plan of action to make observing Taharat HaMishpachah feasible. My hometown did not have a mikveh; the nearest one was in Chernowitz, eighty kilometers away."

Shortly after the birth of Mrs. Krovsky's first daughter, the mikveh and the adjoining shul in Chernowitz were closed down. Desperate inquiries led to the discovery of an "officially permitted" mikveh in Lemberg, 115 kilometers away. Mrs. Krovsky would go to work in the morning as usual, then travel to Lemberg by bus or train in the afternoon. "I had to make the return trip late the same night in order to report to work the next morning on time. Otherwise, people would begin asking questions.

"These were considered 'ideal conditions.' The real difficulties started when the Lemberg mikveh was also shut down. We turned back to Chernowitz where a group of dedicated Jews tried to reopen an old mikveh dating back to pre-war times. This mikveh was located in the basement of a private home. Its owner, a Jewish woman, was reluctant to endanger herself and others by allowing access to the much sought-after pool in her basement. Many hours of imploring and pleading and, of course, the promise of a handsome fee finally persuaded her to agree.

"*The next step was to repair the old mikveh and prepare it for use. All the construction had to be carried out in maximum secrecy and silence. We could not risk talkative neighbors. The woman would not allow us to build an entrance from her home. The only way to get in was by crawling through a hole in the basement wall.*

"*Despite the generous sum of money the house owner received, she would not allow the use of the mikveh on Sundays and public holidays. On these days, she ran an active 'black market' in her home, and she didn't want visitors to inquire about the strange figures emerging from the cellar.*

"*Still, we insisted on using the mikveh on those days, promising to stay out of sight of her customers. I remember many an anxious hour, waiting patiently by the exit, praying that the last buyer would leave in time for me to make the last train home.*"

Years passed, and another old basement mikveh became available in the center of town. At first, the water was heated by a boiler, but tenants complained about the unexplainable rise in the electric bill. For fear of discovery, the electric wiring to the mikveh was disconnected. "*I don't have to tell you how cold water can get in the freezing Russian winter. We were forced to heat up water on gas stoves upstairs and carry it down to the basement, tens of buckets each time.*"

When this was no longer feasible, Mrs. Krovsky tried a different alternative, a 450-kilometer trip across the Carpathian mountains to the city of Ungrod. Sometimes she was lucky enough to make the trip by plane. Usually, she would fly one way and take a bus home. "*I still shudder at the thought of those late-night bus rides among the primitive Russian peasants.*

"*When we could afford a vacation to the big cities — Moscow, Leningrad, or Kiev — I had the opportunity to use the local mikveh. It was sad to behold the small number of women who took advantage of the mikveh. Many were afraid to come lest they be questioned — even the attendants could have been informers.*

"Thank G-d, that's all past history. Here in Eretz Yisrael, I can fulfill the vital mitzvah of Taharat HaMishpachah in comfort and ease. Do you still wonder why I am tearful?"

The Russian woman's story can be retold with different names and in different places — wherever there is a Jewish woman determined to maintain the practice of *Taharat HaMishpachah.*

IN SOUTHERN SPAIN, a small port city located between mountain and sea lies basking in the Mediterranean sun. The peaceful vacation atmosphere of this resort town belies the constant struggle of one observant Jewish family to keep Torah and mitzvot, and to share our singular heritage with other Jews. Their house is always full of guests, and many travelers to Spain have returned home inspired to seek out their Jewish heritage because of the experience they shared with the Gold family.

In addition to the lack of suitable schools, kosher food, and active synagogue, there is no mikveh. Regular flights to France with a nursing infant are not affordable, besides the fact that there are five other young children at home. The only alternative is the sea. Spain's beaches are extremely inviting on hot, sunny, summer days, but nighttime dipping (especially in the winter) is not everyone's delight. Nevertheless, once a month Mrs. Gold makes her way across the sandy beach, prepared to endure the chilly waters, and all the while careful to abide by the specific laws the Rav has given her regarding using the sea for immersion.

Even under conditions of freedom, acceptance, and affluence, adhering to the dictates of *Taharat HaMishpachah* can prove to be a challenge — a point Mrs. Gold could freely attest to. The stories of women who have persevered in the face of great hardship may appear to dwarf our own difficulties, but each woman can relate her own stories of heroic determination and unswerving commitment to fulfill G-d's will.

The Jewish woman has been charged with the responsibility for the maintenance of this fundamental mitzvah. While there are laws and prohibitions, such as observing the *harchakot*, the laws of separation, for which the husband, too, is responsible, the practical observance of this mitzvah — checking her body, immersing in the *mikveh*, and keeping a calendar — is entrusted solely to the Jewish woman. No one is instructed to verify or check her actions. Her word is relied upon absolutely, and halachic decisions are based on information which she provides.

The Jewish woman deserves this trust. Not only because it's her body which is involved, but also because G-d esteems women's ability to keep the Torah.

> *Thus shall you say to the house of Yaakov and tell to the children of Israel.*
>
> *(Shemot 19:3)*

"The house of Yaakov" refers to the Jewish women. We see that Moshe Rabbeinu was instructed to teach the Torah to them before the men. Why the women first? Because they are quick to do mitzvot (*Midrash Rabbah* on *Parashat Yitro* 28:2). Commentators explain, "They accept with faith and without doubting and investigation."

RABBI LEVI YITZCHAK OF BERDITCHEV was famous for his constant efforts to find merit in and glorify his Jewish brethren. Once, on the day before Pesach, he sent his attendant in search of a pint of beer. The attendant knocked on the doors of the freshly cleaned Jewish homes and stated his request.

"What?" came the replies. "Beer! Beer is chametz! Tonight is Pesach, and I have already cleaned my home. G-d forbid we should possess a drop of chametz at this hour!" The attendant returned empty-handed to Rabbi Levi Yitzchak.

But Rabbi Levi Yitzchak seemed rather pleased. He sent the attendant out once again, this time to fetch a bit of tobacco from any one of the Jews in the village. Government officials had recently forbid possession of tobacco and threatened to imprison anyone found with it. To enforce their edict, they would make surprise searches among the villagers.

Nevertheless, the attendant had little difficulty obtaining this forbidden item. He handed Rabbi Levi Yitzchak the package, but instead of smoking the tobacco, Rabbi Levi Yitzchak waved it towards the heavens. Lifting his eyes and with a beaming look of pride on his face, he exclaimed, "G-d, see how precious Your commandments are to Your children! The government posts soldiers to enforce its rules and regulations, yet see how easily I was able to procure this tobacco. Almost four thousand years ago, You commanded the Jewish people to rid their homes of chametz. Today, not a drop could be found! Your people keep Your commandments sincerely without any pressure or force."

It is part of the pride of our heritage that no matter how complex or difficult the keeping of a mitzvah may be, the Jewish people have demonstrated incredible integrity in their standards of observance. The trust the Torah places in women in the matter of the vital area of *Taharat HaMishpachah* is an indication of how highly the Torah regards them.

The Torah has placed a great responsibility in the hands of women. However, this responsibility should not create undue anxiety or tension. A joyful approach to observing the rules of *Taharat HaMishpachah* invites the *Shechinah*, the Divine Presence, to descend upon the couple.

When a man and woman merit it, the Shechinah rests between them.

(Sotah 17a)

The letters of the Hebrew word for woman, *ishah*, contain the word *eish*, meaning fire. The letters of the word *ish*, the Hebrew for man, also contain *eish* — fire. The two remaining letters contained in each of their names, *yud* and *heh*, combine to form G-d's name, *Yud-Heh*. When a man and a woman approach marriage in the proper way, the Divine Presence rests between them, but if they remove G-dliness (G-d's name) from their marriage, they are left with fire — *eish*. Their marriage will be as vulnerable as dry straw before a flame. Our Sages declared, "The *Shechinah* rests only in an atmosphere of joy" (*Shabbat* 30b). The Talmud encourages a couple to fulfill the mitzvot associated with *Taharat HaMishpachah* with happiness and joy. In this manner, G-dliness becomes a very real force in our lives, not only in the synagogue, or in those areas of life which we consider holy, but in every aspect of our life experience.

MRS. BERNSTEIN is an observant woman. In addition to managing her home and caring for her children, she has established a growing business as an interior decorating consultant. Stressing sensitivity and the personal touch, she involves herself in her clients' needs and requirements by sharing her insights on the best ways to set up a Jewish home.

She recalls one particular woman who was impressed with this professional, yet personal, approach. As the two women chatted over tea, Mrs. Bernstein suggested a variety of attractive decorating plans.

Their conversation continued, as Mrs. Bernstein described to her client the transformation of a house into a home. She stressed

the importance and impact that proper decor can have on creat-
ing a Jewish atmosphere within the walls of the home.

"Every part of the home, from the kitchen to the dining room
to the children's room, can have a special Jewish atmosphere. For
example, we can make a corner for the books with a place for your
husband to study Torah with your children. This corner will be
the most beautiful place — a sanctuary to G-d."

Mrs. Bernstein continued: "I've drawn up a plan for your
bedroom with two separate beds. Our Sages stated, 'When man
and woman merit, the Divine Presence rests between them.' If a
couple want G-d's Presence in their house, they must make room
for it in every place."

The rules of *Taharat HaMishpachah* are designed to sustain
and preserve the original bond that began under the marriage
canopy. While a woman is a *niddah,* she does not have intimate relations with her husband. This period of physical separation is accompanied by psychological and spiritual
preparation and, finally, sanctification, as she immerses in the
mikveh. Only then may marital relations be resumed. One of
the greatest dangers to marriage is boredom. When a couple
keep the laws of *Taharat HaMishpachah,* they prevent this phenomenon and enable renewal to take place each month.

There are those who claim that even from a purely medical
perspective, observing *Taharat HaMishpachah* can be beneficial. Research shows that, generally, a woman's vaginal discharge is mildly acidic and therefore antiseptic. In contrast, at
the time of her period, this discharge is alkaline, and it takes
approximately seven days to regain its normal pH. Thus, during this time when a woman is a *niddah,* the vagina lacks its
natural protection and the possibility of infection rises.

Furthermore, at the time of menstruation, the uterine lining
has been shed and the entire uterine channel resembles an open

wound. This leaves it susceptible to the entrance of germs. It takes seven days after the end of the period for the lining to become firm and strong again. Intimate relations during the time the Torah defines as *niddah* may then prove harmful.

Finally, a number of medical studies of the incidence of cervical cancer show that it can occur as much as twenty times more frequently among women who don't practice *Taharat HaMishpachah* than among those who do.

> *I am G-d who heals you.*
>
> *(Shemot 15:26)*

G-d has given us the Torah's guidelines as a way of life and has promised that fulfilling its commandments will lead to a lifetime of health and prosperity. Nevertheless, we must remember that the reasons for observing the mitzvot are not the benefits we will reap from them, but because they are G-d's will.

While the observance of *Taharat HaMishpachah* makes sense medically as well as psychologically, the very name *Taharat HaMishpachah* — Family Purity — would imply that its merit extends far beyond these two areas. It is not called *Taharat HaIshah*, "woman's purity," despite its obvious connection with a woman's cycle. Not just the woman herself, but her immediate and extended family, the entire Jewish nation and its future generations, are directly influenced by the purity and wholesomeness which the Divine plan inspires.

> *Rav Chalaftah declared: "How fortunate is the woman! How fortunate is the mother! How fortunate is the family of any woman who keeps the laws properly.*
>
> *(Breita, Niddah 4:1)*

Taharat HaMishpachah is influential in molding the spiritual nature and well-being of our children. We all want the best for our offspring. Keeping *Taharat HaMishpachah* is something we can do for them even before conception.

ROOM 312 ON the third floor of Rambam Hospital in Haifa was occupied by two middle-aged Israeli men: Mr. Ben-Shalom, the secretary of one of Israel's more successful kibbutzim, and a well-known rabbi.

They spent many hours in conversation. The rabbi was impressed with his roommate's popularity. It seemed that everyone on the kibbutz came to visit him. Two young men, in particular, attracted his attention. They visited frequently, and Mr. Ben-Shalom seemed very pleased to see them.

They appeared so different from the others. Mr Ben-Shalom's kibbutz belonged to Kibbutz HaArtzi, the secular-left kibbutz movement. These youths wore kippot on their heads and sported unshaven sideburns and tzitzit. Where did they meet Mr. Ben-Shalom? How did the apparent closeness between them develop?

One day, the rabbi could not contain his curiosity any longer. "Excuse me for being so nosy," he remarked to Mr. Ben-Shalom, "but who are those two young Orthodox fellows who visit you so often?"

Mr. Ben-Shalom smiled and propped his cushions up behind him. "They're two of the kibbutz's prize products, but to understand how this came to be is a long story."

The rabbi turned to his friend attentively, and Mr. Ben-Shalom continued:

"During the Holocaust," he began, "a mother and daughter, the sole survivors of an entire family, were deported to a Nazi death camp. They clung together as their train was unloaded. Some passengers were sent to the gas chambers immediately, others to the barracks.

"As the mother was torn away from her daughter, she im-

plored her: 'Promise me that if you survive and live to marry and build a home, you will keep Taharat HaMishpachah.'

"With tears in her eyes, the girl vowed to fulfill her mother's last wish. She had no idea of their meaning, but she repeated the words 'Taharat HaMishpachah' over and over again, engraving them in her mind, lest she forget. She sensed their message as her only connection to a world that no longer existed...

"What she endured, how she endured, is too long a story, but she made it. When the war was over, she was sent to Israel by the Jewish Agency Committee for Refugees. Here, she was placed in our kibbutz and soon acclimated herself to her new life.

"Years passed. She was about to marry one of the kibbutz members. It was then that she remembered her mother's last wish. The words 'Taharat HaMishpachah' echoed in her ears, and she was determined to keep the promise she had made.

" 'I hope you will agree to my condition,' she said to him, relating her vow. 'I don't even know what 'Taharat HaMishpachah' is, but I have decided to keep it!'

"Impressed with her sincerity, he agreed, and the girl set about seeking an explanation on the subject. She received individual instruction and learned the detailed laws. The more she learned, the happier she felt with her decision. Sensing a new connection with her long-gone family, her past, and her people's history, she approached marriage with confidence and joy.

"The couple continued to live on the kibbutz. Nothing differentiated them from the other members except for a deep and lasting commitment to the observance of Taharat HaMishpachah."

Mr. Ben-Shalom paused. His roommate eyed him curiously, sensing there was more to come.

"You see, my friend," he continued, *"that Holocaust survivor is my wife, and those two boys are our sons. They are the envy of all my friends. All are impressed by their refinement, character,*

and their desire for meaning and direction in life. Everyone respects them for their observant lifestyle. I believe it has something to do with the commitment my wife and I made."

Chapter 3

Getting to Know the Divine Image within You

His head is as the most fine gold, his locks are wavy, black as a raven's.

(Shir HaShirim 5:11)

OUR SAGES NOTED THAT the Hebrew word for raven, *orev*, resembles the Hebrew for sweet, *arev*. They commented: There are certain passages of the Torah, for example, the laws of *niddah*, which may appear too ugly and black to teach publicly. Nevertheless, G-d declares:

To Me, they are as sweet as fine gold.

(Vayikra Rabbah 19:3)

The laws of *niddah* require a familiarity with intimate details. That these details should be discussed, and in the open at that, can be an uncomfortable thought. Nevertheless, G-d treasures the study and examination of them, because only through such study is it possible to fulfill the laws properly.

What Is the Law of a Niddah?

The Torah states that a woman becomes *teme'ah*, ritually

impure, when she experiences her menstrual period, and prohibits intimacy with a woman while she is in this state.

> *You shall not approach a woman in her time of menstrual*
> *impurity to uncover her nakedness...do not become impure*
> *with all these, for with all these did the nations I expel before*
> *you become impure.*
>
> (*Vayikra* 18:19, 24)

The Torah prescribes the punishment of *karet* for violation of this prohibition, the same punishment that is prescribed for a person who, G-d forbid, eats on Yom Kippur or who is not circumcised.

Tumah, ritual impurity, and *taharah*, ritual purity, are spiritual concepts.

> *It is clear that the laws of ritual purity and impurity are decrees*
> *of the Torah that cannot be comprehended by human wisdom.*
>
> (Rambam, Hilchot Mikvaot 11:12)

In no manner or form can they be identified with physical cleanliness and its opposite. Before immersing herself in the *mikveh*, a woman cleanses herself thoroughly. Nevertheless, to become ritually pure, she must immerse in the *mikveh's* waters. Similarly, the High Priest would immerse himself in the *mikveh* five times on Yom Kippur. Surely these immersions were not required because he was dirty!

The laws of *Taharat HaMishpachah* are designed to be in harmony with a woman's physical, emotional, spiritual, and psychological makeup. They allow and require her to be "in touch" with herself in a very real and conscious manner.

When Does a Woman Enter the State of Niddah?

Any woman — even if she be pregnant, nursing, or past

menopause — who discovers a discharge of blood which originated from her uterus, enters the state of *niddah*. This applies whether the discharge occurs at a time when she would normally expect her period or not. Uterine bleeding resulting from birth or a gynecologist's examination also renders a woman a *niddah*. So does hymenal bleeding (even though it is not from the uterus).

A woman must be aware of the laws governing this subject so that she will be knowledgeable enough to detect the possibility of her being a *niddah*. G-d placed the responsibility of observing the laws of *Taharat HaMishpachah* in the woman's hands. She must know well the details of the laws which determine when she becomes a *niddah* and when she is *tehorah*, i.e., not a *niddah*.

Nevertheless, meeting this responsibility requires the assistance and guidance of a Rav. In addition to his halachic knowledge, a Rav will have developed the sensitivity required for dealing with these delicate and personal issues. A woman must have a Rav with whom she feels comfortable to consult when questions arise.

How Does One Determine the State of Niddah?

Torah law distinguishes between two types of discharges:

> 1. A *mareh*, in which the discharge is accompanied by a *hargashah*, specific physical sensation, i.e., the woman feels the opening of the uterus or she feels the passage of liquid passing through the vagina.
>
> 2. A *ketem*, in which a stain is discovered without any prior sensation.

A *mareh* always renders a woman a *niddah*. Even the tiniest drop of blood coming from the uterus places a woman in that state. In contrast, there are certain leniencies in regard to *ketamim*, stains. The stains must be brought to a Rav who will decide the matter according to criteria discussed later.

Blood which is discovered on a *bedikah* cloth in the process of a *bedikah*, an internal inspection, is considered equivalent to a *mareh*. (See ch. 5 for a description of a *bedikah* cloth.)

Our Sages determined two criteria for defining the term *hargashah*, physical sensation:

1. a sensation of the opening of the uterus (it is very rare for a woman to be able to distinguish this feeling nowadays);

2. the feeling of liquid passing through the vagina.

A woman who experiences either of these sensations is required to do a *bedikah*, an internal inspection, shortly afterwards by means of a *bedikah* cloth in order to verify whether the feeling was connected with uterine bleeding or not. (How the *bedikah* is performed is explained in ch. 5.)

If she discovers blood, she becomes a *niddah*. If she discovers a secretion whose color clearly indicates that it is not blood, she is *tehorah*. If she does not discover any secretion at all, she should consult a Rav.

This *bedikah* does not have to be made by women who are *mesulakot damim* — i.e., women who are more than three months pregnant, women who have not menstruated while nursing, or women who are past menopause.

Similarly, a woman who frequently experiences vaginal discharges other than blood may avoid the need for these internal inspections by creating a *chazakah*, which is proof that her discharges are *tahor*. She does this by carrying out the following procedure:

On three successive occasions, shortly after the sensation of liquid passing through the vagina, the woman should make a *bedikah*. If she discovers secretions which are *tahor*, she may rest assured that, in her case, this sensation is not necessarily related to the onset of menstruation.

With this procedure, a woman establishes that her vaginal discharges are normally not blood. Hence, she is never required to check for uterine bleeding after experiencing such a sensation again unless it occurs on the days on which she might expect her menstrual period.

Determining the Nature of a Vaginal Discharge

A discharge of a color other than white, blue, or green may render a woman a *niddah*. In the event of the discovery of discharges of questionable colors, she should consult a Rav to determine her status. It is not sufficient to consult one's husband or a friend, even if they are somewhat knowledgeable concerning these matters.

Staining

A woman may discover a *ketem*, stain, of a questionable color resembling blood without experiencing any sensation associated with vaginal discharge. This might render her a *niddah*, and she must consult a Rav to determine her status. It is preferable to consult the Rav as soon as possible.

Among the factors which are important in facilitating the Rav's decision are:

1. where the stain was found: on the woman's body (where on the body?), on her clothes (where on the clothes? were they white or colored? outer clothes or underclothes?), on her sheets (were they white or colored?), or on another place;

2. the color of the stain;

3. the cleanliness of the place where the stain was found;

4. the possibility of attributing the stain to external factors (e.g., a mother treating a child's nosebleed, or a mosquito bite, or preparation of red-colored foods);

5. the size of the stain.

A *ketem* can only render a woman a *niddah* if it is at least a *gris* in size. The latter measurement is the size of a circle approximately nineteen millimeters in diameter. However, it is rare to find stains so conveniently circular. The particular rules of measuring the size of a different shaped stain, what to do when two smaller stains are discovered next to each other, and other particular questions make the guidance of a Rav a necessity.

It must be emphasized that the above applies to stains discovered on the body or on clothes without experiencing any sensations associated with vaginal discharge. When a stain is discovered on a *bedikah* cloth, more stringent rules apply, and even the tiniest drop of blood can render a woman a *niddah*.

General Rules Regarding Stains

1. Do not make internal inspections after discovering a stain unless instructed to do so by a Rav.

2. It is a good idea to wear colored underpants when *tehorah*. This minimizes the possibility that any given stain will render a woman a *niddah*.

3. Do not inspect toilet paper after use.

4. Stains are not regarded as contributing factors in calculating *onot perishah* (see ch. 10).

Gynecological Examinations[1]

Uterine bleeding resulting from a gynecologist's internal examination renders a woman a *niddah*. Furthermore, in certain instances, this examination may render a woman a *niddah* even if no bleeding is apparent. This matter can only be decided by a Rav. However, awareness of the nature of the examination can greatly assist a woman and her Rav in determining her status. It is suggested that these guidelines be followed:

1. A gynecologist's examinations should ideally be scheduled for the time when a woman is a *niddah* and before she makes a *hefsek taharah*, confirmation of the end of menstrual flow (see ch. 5).

2. Inquire about the nature and necessity of the examination beforehand.

3. After the examination, request complete details about the procedure. In particular, if a wound is discovered, find out its exact location.

4. A manual examination which does not cause the opening of the uterus does not make a woman a *niddah*. Examinations using certain instruments may cause the opening up of the uterus and, thus, render a woman a *niddah*. In order to make a decision on this matter, a Rav must be informed which instruments were used.

5. Needless to say, a gynecologist's opinion without the confirmation of a rabbinic authority may not be relied upon in determining a woman's *niddah* status.

Situations that require consultation with both medical and

---

1. A woman must be careful not to be alone (in *yichud*) with a male doctor. She should consult a Rav regarding how to conduct herself when visiting a male doctor.

halachic authorities include:

   a) blood found in urine;

   b) a sore in the vaginal area;

   c) cervical erosion or other internal bleeding;

   d) midcycle bleeding and staining.

The Role of the Rav

The Rav is accustomed to dealing with the subject of *Taharat HaMishpachah* in a sensitive fashion, conscious of the delicacy of the issues involved and concerned for the woman's need for privacy. Some of the questions he asks may cause some embarrassment or seem unduly personal, but how different is this from talking to a gynecologist?

By nature, we women find it unpleasant when we have to visit a gynecologist, but we go. We realize that our physical health is at stake and that the gynecologist is a professional, whose intention is to help. Consequently, we overcome whatever embarrassment we feel when talking to him.

The same should apply to an even greater extent when talking to a Rav. He is dedicated to our spiritual well-being, and his questions are asked with the sole purpose of verifying facts in order to be of service to us. The thought that a learned scholar, trained in the service of G-d and anxious to help his fellow man, is willing to give us his time and attention should be a source of reassurance and satisfaction. Thus, there is no place for hesitation or shame in asking the Rav any questions. Rather, we should be matter-of-fact in our approach, providing all the information needed.

There is a further point necessary to remember in this context. A Rav is trained to assist a woman in maintaining a state of *taharah* and to declare her a *niddah* only when according to the halachah she is not *tahor*. There is a need for strict and careful adherence to the *niddah* laws, but there is no need for stringencies that go beyond those required by the halachah.

A woman's state of *niddah* is an unavoidable reality of life. However, the *niddah* state does have its own specific advantages. It protects a woman physically and emotionally and gives her time for self-rejuvenation and an opportunity for spiritual growth, as we have discussed.

Nevertheless, when the physical situation allows, the Torah does not want the woman to abstain when in the state of *taharah* from the abundance of physical and spiritual well-being that her days of *taharah* bring.

A Rav is trained to know when stringency is required and when it is out of place. We must rely on his judgement and realize that he is trying to arrive at a halachic decision that is in our own best interests and in harmony with the workings of our bodies. A proper attitude on our part can greatly assist him in guiding us.

Consulting a Rav Is Both a Requirement and an Advantage

1. Only a Rav can determine the status of spots and stains of a questionable type, size, or coloring.

2. A Rav can be helpful when problems arise which are related to difficulties in becoming pregnant.

3. A Rav can advise a woman who has difficulty in making *bedikot*, internal inspections.

4. A Rav can provide Torah-oriented counseling in cases of marital difficulties.

5. Refraining from consulting a Rav is not considered an act of modesty. Quite the contrary, one must never re-

frain from seeking advice and asking questions.

6. When consulting a Rav, a woman should state her question clearly, providing all the necessary information.

Typical Information to Keep in Mind When Consulting a Rav

What day of her cycle did the woman discover the discharge? Was she *tehorah*? Was it the day she was expecting her period (see ch. 10)? Was the discharge found after the *hefsek taharah* (see ch. 5)? Was it on the *hefsek taharah bedikah* cloth? Was it on the *moch dachuk* (see ch. 5)? What was its size? Were any of the following conditions involved: pregnancy, nursing, childbirth, a gynecologist's examination, gynecological problems, fertility problems? Does the question regard a *bedikah* cloth? Was it checked to verify cleanliness before use? Does the question regard a garment? White or colored? Of synthetic or natural material? Did she feel the passage of liquid? Is she a bride prior to her wedding or newly married? Was the staining found after marital relations? After urinating? If yes, how soon after? Does she have a hemorrhoid problem?

Whenever a question arises which may render a woman a *niddah*, she must refrain from physical contact with her husband until she receives the Rav's decision. Needless to say, she should never regard a question lightly and consider herself *tehorah* without proper halachic determination. However, neither should she consider herself a *niddah* in order to save herself the inconvenience of consulting with a Rav.

Chapter 4

The Spotless Week

THE HIGH PRIEST in the Holy Temple was garbed in splendid clothing. Multicolored threads, hand woven into a magnificent garment, and ornamental bells adorning his robe underscored the unique position which he occupied in the service of G-d.

When the High Priest entered the Holy Temple, the ringing of the bells about his robe would announce his arrival. Our Sages drew a parallel from the behavior of the High Priest in the Temple to that of every person in his "miniature sanctuary" — his own private home. They counseled the following: "Do not enter your home suddenly" (*Pesachim* 112a). The Rashbam brings the midrash in *Vayikra Rabbah*: "Every person should emulate the High Priest's example and make others aware of his presence before entering his home."

Indeed, this idea can take on an additional significance when talking about a woman. When a woman begins married life and commits herself to the observance of *Taharat HaMishpachah,* she must not "enter suddenly." One cannot simply burst into this lifestyle without proper preparation.

Before and after the marriage ceremony, it is our privilege and obligation to study and learn the detailed laws of *Taharat HaMishpachah*. We as women are aware of the many different facets, functions, moods, and capabilities that are so characteristic of our femininity. The detailed laws of *Taharat HaMishpachah* reflect our many-sided nature. Through the study of these laws, we learn to understand ourselves better and gain greater awareness of the plan G-d designed for married life.

> *AN ELECTRICIAN WAS CALLED upon to install the electricity in a new building. He arrived promptly and set to work on the wires. After working for a short time connecting wires here and putting in switches there, he announced that his work was completed.*
>
> *"But surely you couldn't have finished the job so quickly!" exclaimed the customer. "I'm not very familiar with this wiring, but I do believe you did your job in record time."*
>
> *"Sure," replied the electrician with confidence. "I'm an expert. I know what I'm doing." However, his pleasure was short-lived and his smile turned to a frown when he tried to switch on the unit. It didn't work!*
>
> *"What do you say to this?" demanded the customer.*
>
> *The electrician shrugged. "Sorry to disappoint you, sir. Look, I did connect the main wires. As for some of the small wires — well, you see, I'm just not a fanatic for details."*

We must approach *Taharat HaMishpachah* earnestly. "Getting the general idea" or "doing what I understand" is not sufficient. When a tiny wire is disconnected, an entire electrical unit will not function. Similarly, if a woman ignores even a seemingly slight aspect of the laws of *Taharat HaMishpachah*, she may completely invalidate the whole process of purification.

Taharat HaMishpachah should bring us happiness, satisfaction, and inner peace. However, by no means should the comfort and relaxation we feel in its observance give way to casualness or carelessness.

A woman who seeks stringencies, where the Torah has not commanded this, clinging to *her* conception of the laws, is as mistaken as the woman who keeps the laws carelessly, ignoring basic elements of their performance, because they both share the same fundamental error: neither is committed to keeping the mitzvah according to the halachah. Both allow their own conception (or misconception) of what *Taharat HaMishpachah* is to control their behavior. (Of course, a woman may choose to take upon herself certain accepted stringencies, with the concurrence of her husband.)

We must commit ourselves to the study and review of these laws so that we understand them in their totality and are able to fulfill them as G-d desires.

Lacking the knowledge of fine details can also be the cause of much unnecessary discomfort and hardship.

MIRIAM WAS A YOUNG newlywed. She felt a sense of growth and development as she confronted the challenges of married life. She felt confident and happy, ready and eager to create a pleasant atmosphere in her meticulously kept home.

She found herself, however, in a difficult predicament. Here she was, six weeks after her wedding, and she was still unable to go the mikveh again. Miriam, who had studied the laws of Taharat HaMishpachah prior to her marriage, tried in vain to recall a chapter that dealt with a situation similar to hers. Unable to do so, she made her own halachic decisions, for despite the fact that she had learned that one should consult a Rav whenever a question arose, Miriam was adamant in her refusal to ask a Rav!

*She had accepted upon herself the full observance of this com-
mandment, but what seemed to her the embarrassing step of asking a Rav a question — that not!*

*Desperately, she turned to a friend for guidance. The friend in-
troduced Miriam to an experienced Taharat HaMishpachah counselor. In a patient manner, the woman discussed the issues with
Miriam and convinced her to make an appointment with a Rav.*

*After speaking to the Rav, Miriam was very sorry she hadn't
done so before. The Rav informed her that she hadn't been a
niddah for all this time and that she could have gone to the
mikveh. All the aggravation she and her husband had gone
through could easily have been prevented and certainly was unnecessary!*

*But not entirely for nothing. Call it "learning the hard way,"
if you will. Miriam finally understood that she ought not to rely
on her own judgment, but should call a Rav when a problem
arises.*

Miriam is not alone. Many women who are committed to
the practice of *Taharat HaMishpachah* are unaware of the detailed aspects of the laws. Therefore, it is advisable for a
woman to find a Rav (or *Taharat HaMishpachah* counselor)
with whom she feels comfortable discussing any questions
which may arise.

Indeed, after a woman marries, it is advisable for her to pe-
riodically review the laws of *Taharat HaMishpachah*. Because
of the detailed nature of these laws, we are likely to forget or
overlook certain aspects of them as time passes. Also, when a
woman is pregnant or exclusively nursing, she generally does
not enter the state of *niddah*. These long intervals, in which the
laws are not put into practice, may lead to forgetting many
particulars.

Among the other reasons for continued review of these laws are:

1. *Taharat HaMishpachah* is a private and intimate topic. When the laws and concepts were first presented, we may have shied away from asking questions to clarify points that seemed unclear. As we become more familiar and comfortable with the laws, we may find it easier to communicate our questions and observations.

2. These laws were taught to us before marriage, when we lacked the opportunity to observe the practical application of many of these concepts. As we gain more experience in observing *Taharat HaMishpachah*, a review may prove very helpful, for we will now have firsthand knowledge of what were before only theoretical terms.

3. A bride-to-be is very preoccupied with wedding preparations and the redefinition of her personality which marriage entails. Frequently, by the time she sits down to study with a *Taharat HaMishpachah* counselor, she is emotionally and physically drained. This is obviously not the ideal state of mind to be in to fully comprehend complex laws!

4. In previous generations, a mother would teach observance of *Taharat HaMishpachah* to her daughter in a direct, personal, and loving way. In contrast, many women today acquire familiarity with the subject only through classes, books, and lectures. None of these methods is as satisfactory as the personal approach. There is no way we can totally compensate for the loss of the unique opportunity of a mother-daughter teaching situation. Learning individually with a *Taharat HaMishpachah* counselor is the only method which comes close to the mother-daughter arrangement of previous generations.

5. In different communities, there are certain practices that are connected with the laws of *Taharat HaMishpachah*. Many misconceptions can arise out of the confusion of these practices with Torah and Rabbinic law, so a clear distinction must be made. Adequate review will allow a woman to distinguish between those practices which are absolute requirements and those which are not required by law.

SARAH HAD BEEN MARRIED for seven years. Both she and her husband desperately desired children. As a consequence, her failure to become pregnant had made her extremely anxious.

A chance meeting with a friend resulted in her friend suggesting that Sarah join a study group for review of the laws of Taharat HaMishpachah.

"Who me?" Sarah retorted with a touch of bitterness in her voice. "I'm so careful and particular with the laws. Besides, pregnancy and nursing haven't interrupted my monthly visits to the mikveh. I'm an expert by now!"

Nevertheless, after some gentle coaxing, she agreed to attend the class. Much to her amazement, Sarah discovered that a certain self-imposed, stringent manner of her observance was not in accordance with the law.

With the counselor's encouragement, Sarah resolved to increase her knowledge of the laws and find out what she was supposed to do. She consulted a Rav for guidance and followed his instructions. The more she learned, the more she became aware of how wrong she had been.

Indeed, shortly after, Sarah became pregnant. Had she only kept the laws as they were meant to be kept, perhaps she would have merited this earlier.

The stress on detailed study certainly does not mean that a woman should try to become a Rav. Through her study, however, she can and should obtain an awareness of which information is important to a Rav and what factors will be helpful to him in his decision-making process. Often, the knowledge of these factors can make a world of difference.

MRS. BLAU IS AN EXPERIENCED teacher of Taharat HaMishpachah. Here is her own account of a situation in which lack of knowledge of details caused one bride to be unnecessarily anxious.

"It was a pleasant spring evening. My husband and I were driving out to the suburbs to join some friends for their house-warming celebration.

"As we passed through the city, my husband suddenly exclaimed, 'Oh, I almost forgot. Tonight is the wedding of the son of one of my acquaintances. I didn't really plan on going, but since it's not out of our way, let's stop in just to wish them mazel tov!'

"I felt a little awkward entering the wedding hall. I didn't know anyone there. Or at least I thought I didn't.

"Much to my surprise, a woman whose face looked familiar literally ran up to me. I recognized her as a new Taharat HaMishpachah counselor whom I had met at a teachers' convention.

" 'Mrs. Blau,' she called. 'You cannot imagine how happy I am to see you here. I didn't know you were invited, but, never mind, you have arrived as if G-d sent you.'

"I could not imagine what this was all about, but she didn't keep me wondering for long. 'You see,' the counselor continued worriedly, 'the bride just discovered a stain that renders her a niddah! Can you imagine? Right before the chupah!

" 'I've become very close to her during our sessions, and she begged me to properly organize the procedure for tonight. I know there are arrangements to be made, but this has never happened

*to me before, and though I know the law involved, I could use
your assistance.'*

"*As I was pondering the issue, I instinctively asked the counselor what circumstances had rendered the bride a niddah.*

"*As soon as the question left my lips, I regretted it. Who was I
to doubt the counselor? Wouldn't she feel slighted? But my experience with overlooked details dictated that I ask. I inquired further as to the manner in which the question was presented to the
Rav who had decided that the bride was a niddah.*

"*The counselor was only too eager for my involvement, and
we discussed the matter in detail. I quickly realized that the question had not been posed properly; were the Rav to be given a cor-
rected version, with important details that had been omitted, a
different decision might be made.*

"*Sure enough, when the question was rephrased and the bride
herself spoke to the Rav, mentioning additional details, the Rav
changed his decision: The bride was not a niddah. After all this,
how could I not share in the joy of this bride and groom even
though I didn't know them?*

"*As we continued our drive to our original destination, I
found myself saying out loud: 'Thank G-d for details…'*

"*My husband gave me a quizzical glance, but I merely
shrugged. 'Oh it's not important. It's just that, at times, what
you don't know can hurt you.' "*

The above story is an instructive example of the critical
role of small details in the observance of this mitzvah.

The very fact that the laws are so detailed and multifac-
eted can often convince a person of their extreme
importance.

SHARON IS A WOMAN in her late thirties who has been keep-

ing Taharat HaMishpacha for sixteen years. Her observance would not seem at all unusual if it were not for the fact that, for much of that time, her husband took no interest whatsoever in these practices.

"I admire you, and I sense we have a special marriage, so I'm willing to go along with it," he would frequently tell his wife. "But that's it. I'm not interested in learning and understanding the laws. I'll do whatever you want, but after a full day's work, there are other things to which I want to devote whatever mental energy I have left."

Sharon persisted stubbornly. She was convinced that her husband's becoming aware of the advantages in keeping Taharat HaMishpachah would add a deeper dimension to her marriage. She coaxed and pleaded, but to no avail.

One day, it occurred to her to organize a study group on the subject in her home and schedule the meetings at the times when her husband was home. Sharon casually told her husband about the weekly classes to be held in their living room and requested that he make himself comfortable in the adjoining study, as it was mainly "a topic of interest to women."

That very description aroused his curiosity. The class began the next week with a sizeable attendance. Unbeknownst to the teacher, an additional "student" was listening attentively behind the study door.

The sessions continued weekly, with the teacher explaining the issues in depth and answering a multitude of questions. Sharon's husband was fascinated by what he heard, and he was extremely impressed by how the laws accommodated all levels of human functioning.

"There is a unique blend of universality and personal relevance to these laws," he mused to himself. "On the one hand, they revolve around unchanging, objective principles, yet they also

appear to be tailor-made for every individual, down to the most minute detail."

Sharon sensed the change that was coming over her husband and was only too happy to encourage it. She continues to reap the benefits of her cunning scheme to this day. When she meets friends who are confronting a similar situation – uninvolved husbands – she shares her secret with them (and the advantage of having a study adjoining the living room).

The transition from *niddah* to *taharah*, and the laws which govern this transition, is a fundamental component of the halachot of *Taharat HaMishpachah*. A woman who has entered the state of *niddah* follows a procedure of separation, preparation, and sanctification. While a woman is a *niddah*, she and her husband refrain from physical contact. As will be explained in chapter 6, this allows them the opportunity to express their admiration and devotion to each other in other ways.

During the *niddah* days we are actively preparing ourselves for the time of our *taharah*.

Inspections of the vagina, using a white cotton cloth to insure maximum comfort and efficiency, are at the center of our preparations. These internal inspections are carried out throughout the entire seven spotless day period, right up to the time of our immersion in the *mikveh*. The laws explaining the procedure will be discussed in the following chapter.

These inspections are termed *bedikot*. The cloth we use is called the *bedikah* cloth.

The purpose of the *bedikot* is to detect any possibility of continued bleeding or staining from the uterus that might render a woman a *niddah*. The *bedikot* help us be aware of our functioning.

Taharat HaMishpachah gives us a unique opportunity to serve G-d with our very bodies. Women, like men, are obliged to keep the Torah's commandments. Unlike men, however, they are exempt from fulfilling those positive commandments which involve a time factor.

There are 248 positive commandments. The Hebrew numerical value for that number is *ramach* — the letters *reish*, *mem*, and *chet*. The Hebrew word for uterus is *rechem* — again, the letters *reish*, *chet*, and *mem*. Thus, we see that our very femininity encompasses and, in some way, allows for the fulfillment of all positive commandments — even those from which we are exempt.

This all-encompassing approach requires a careful observance of the laws. If the *hefsek taharah* is not carried out in the proper manner, a woman remains a *niddah*; she cannot immerse herself in the *mikveh* even if she continued counting the seven spotless days afterwards. Think of the repercussions carelessness or lack of knowledge in this matter can bring!

MRS. COHEN HAD BEEN a Taharat HaMishpachah counselor for many years. She had lectured frequently on the subject and had an easygoing but thorough approach to teaching the laws. Once, in the middle of a study session on how to make a hefsek taharah, her presentation was interrupted rather rudely.

"That's nonsense," shouted Mrs. Ben David. "I've been making a hefsek taharah for fifteen years. I have five children. I wasn't taught to do it that way."

The other women were shocked. They all knew Mrs. Ben David as an observant woman. Maybe...

Mrs. Cohen didn't leave them much time to ponder the question. Tactfully, but firmly, she replied: "I respect your practices, but what I am teaching is 100 percent correct. So I'll teach it this way, and af-

ter the lesson, you and I will get together and compare notes."

After the class, Mrs. Ben David sought out Mrs. Cohen. "I didn't want to interrupt you again," she ventured, "but I still say you're wrong. Here's how I do a hefsek."

As Mrs. Cohen heard her description, she felt herself in a very delicate situation. How could she tell this woman who was so sure she was right that she was making a crucial mistake. "You know," she replied, "there are real differences between what you're saying and what I teach. Look, tomorrow morning, I have an appointment with Rav Arieli. Come with me, and we'll ask him to clarify the matter once and for all."

Mrs. Ben David was willing. She respected Rav Arieli very much. She "knew" that he would verify her description of what to do.

After a ten minute discussion, Rav Arieli asked Mrs. Cohen to postpone their meeting. She left while he continued speaking with Mrs. Ben David, who finally emerged from the Rav's office in tears. For fifteen years, she had not been doing a hefsek taharah correctly!

Unfortunately, mistakes of this nature are far too common. One *Taharat HaMishpachah* counselor recounts meeting a woman who for twelve years had made a fundamental mistake. She had counted the *hefsek taharah* as the first of the seven clean days instead of starting the count from the day after the *hefsek*! This means that she had gone to the *mikveh* one day before the time. For twelve years, she had remained a *niddah*!

The *bedikot* can prove beneficial medically, as well. After menstruation, the uterus needs a certain amount of time to renew its inner lining. The *bedikot* will immediately detect if there is anything amiss. Often, a *bedikah* can uncover a health problem even before physical discomfort would lead us to a doctor's office for examination.

AVIGAIL WAS A YOUNG WOMAN of twenty-six, a mother of three children and actively involved in many community affairs. A bundle of energy, she expressed her abilities and skills in many ways. The furthest thought from her mind was illness...

Taharat HaMishpachah was her way of life, and she observed all its aspects with commitment and joy. During one menstrual cycle, as she was preparing to make the transition from the niddah to the taharah state, she detected continuous staining on the bedikah cloth long after it usually stopped. She didn't experience heavy bleeding and would have dismissed it as an internal sore.

However, since the stains prevented her from continuing the process of preparation for immersion in the mikveh, she consulted a Rav. He thought the problem unusual and suggested a doctor's examination.

It was with mixed feelings that Avigail scheduled an appointment. Although she knew it was the right thing to do, she felt that she couldn't be bothered with doctors. If not for the dictates of the laws of Taharat HaMishpachah, she probably would have ignored the whole situation. "As a matter of fact," she explained later, "if not for the bedikot, I would never have detected the staining."

In fact, those bedikot may have saved her life. The doctor's examination revealed a tumor, which was, thank G-d, removed. Today, Avigail is back to her busy life and grateful for every day of health.

She often quotes the doctor who treated her. "You're a very fortunate lady, Avigail. The tumor was discovered while it was in its early stages. We were able to remove it relatively easily and are reasonably sure that it will not reoccur. I wonder what made you come in for a checkup? It seemed as though you almost knew something was wrong. But at that stage, how could you have known?..."

If we dedicate ourselves to keeping these laws and study them thoroughly, G-D will grant us the ability to fulfill them as He intended.

ADINA LIVED IN NEW YORK. She and her family had come to spend the Pesach holidays with her parents in Eretz Yisrael. She had left the USA in the middle of counting the seven spotless days. She didn't give the matter a second thought. She had no idea that differences in hours between countries could raise halachic questions. When packing, Adina questioned whether to take her personal calendar. "No," she thought, "we're only going for a short time. What for?"

The trip was more tiring than usual. Adina's baby kept her up most of the time. Both she and the baby were jet-lagged for a number of days afterwards. Time became a little fuzzy. Adina calculated the days to her immersion by heart and went to immerse in a beautiful mikveh in Jerusalem.

As she was about to leave after her immersion, she caught sight of the calendar hanging on the mikveh door, and it suddenly hit her that because of the time zones, this was the sixth and not the seventh day after the hefsek taharah (chapter 5), and she had to wait another day.

With slight embarrassment, but happy to be able to keep the laws correctly, she returned to immerse the following night.

Adina wanted to fulfill G-D's will and had tried her best – therefore G-D had helped her and had caused her to realize her error.

"Sanctify yourselves, and you will be holy" (*Vayikra* 20:7). Our Sages comment on this verse: "If a person makes the effort to sanctify himself even slightly, G-d will make him holy both in this world and the world to come" (*Yoma* 39). The Vilna Gaon explains that holiness does not descend from heaven; rather, man himself, through his actions, brings about holiness.

RABBI LEVY WAS STUDYING with a colleague when a car pulled up to his door. A woman who was clearly a stranger emerged slowly from the passenger seat of the car and proceeded towards the doorway with an envelope in her hand. She hesitated a moment and then rang the bell. Rabbi Levy answered the door. With a trace of embarrassment, the woman extended the envelope to the Rabbi. In it was a bedikah cloth, and on it were written the details of the internal inspection.

"Is it okay?" the woman asked. "I don't know much about religious law but I keep the laws of Taharat HaMishpachah. The counselor who taught me these laws emphasized the necessity of bringing questionable colors to a Rav. That's why I'm here. It's so important to me to keep this mitzvah perfectly."

Chapter 5

The Countdown

What Is a Hefsek Taharah?

AFTER A WOMAN'S menstrual bleeding has ceased, she must inspect herself to confirm her readiness for the preparation that leads to the change of status from *niddah* to *taharah*.

The *hefsek taharah*, the confirmation of the end of menstrual bleeding, involves an internal inspection of the vagina to check that bleeding from the uterus has entirely ceased. Once a woman has verified this, she may begin counting the *shivah neki'im*, the seven spotless days, from the following day. The day on which the *hefsek taharah* is carried out is not counted as one of the seven spotless days.

When Can a Woman Perform the Hefsek Taharah?

A woman cannot make a *hefsek taharah* until the afternoon of the fifth day after she has entered the state of *niddah*. The day on which her period began is counted as the first of these five days. For this reason, and also to help calculate *onot perishah* (see ch. 10), it is advisable to mark down on a personal calendar the Hebrew date when menstruation began, and whether it began in the daytime or at night, i.e., before or after *sheki'ah*, sunset.[1]

The Hebrew calendar date is from sunset to sunset the following day. For example: If a woman's period began after sunset on Tuesday or any time on Wednesday till before sunset, she cannot make the *hefsek taharah bedikah* until Sunday before sunset.

A woman must wait five days,[2] even if her menstruation ceases before that time. Obviously, a woman with a longer period must wait until her period ends and only then may she perform the *hefsek taharah*.[3]

These five days are required when immediately prior to the onset of menstruation, the woman had been *tehorah*, i.e., not a *niddah*. However, a woman who had already been a *niddah* for five days — for example, because of a stain that was judged as blood — and then her menstrual period commenced, may carry out a *hefsek taharah* as soon as she is able.

For example: On Sunday a woman discovers a stain which a Rav decides renders her a *niddah*. She waits five days, but on Thursday she begins menstruating. Since five days have already passed in the state of *niddah*, she does not have to wait an additional five days from Thursday. If she has a short

1. For a sample of recording in a personal calendar, see page 149.
2. There are woman from *Eidot HaMizrach* who begin counting after four days if the bleeding has completely ceased. Of course, this practice should be followed only according to the decision of a Rav.
3. A woman past menopause, or a pregnant woman, who only then becomes aware of *Taharat HaMishpachah* and commits herself to its observance, must abstain from physical contact with her husband and count five days prior to making the *hefsek taharah bedikah*. Afterwards, as all other women, she must count seven spotless days before immersing in the *mikveh*.

period she may do a *hefsek taharah* as soon as she is able.

The same applies to a woman who discovers a stain, which is determined to be blood, during her seven spotless days. She may perform a new *hefsek taharah* as soon as she is able.

Specific Leniencies

1. A bride-to-be does not have to wait five days from the day she began menstruating when preparing herself for her initial immersion in the *mikveh*. Rather, she is allowed to carry out the *hefsek taharah* as soon as she is able.[4]

2. A newlywed bride who becomes a *niddah* due to hymenal bleeding may carry out a *hefsek taharah* four days after becoming a *niddah* (if she is able).

3. Women who are ovulating before immersing in the *mikveh* and, consequently, are having difficulty becoming pregnant, should consult a Rav. He is trained to offer a number of possible solutions to the problem.

4. A woman who discovers blood after her immersion in the *mikveh* but before resuming marital relations need not wait for five days and may make a *hefsek taharah* as soon as she is able. However, because of the unusual nature of this instance, it is advisable to consult a Rav.

---

4. This leniency does not apply to a bride who before her wedding was unfamiliar with Jewish law — which forbids all physical contact between the couple prior to the wedding — and who was not abstaining from physical relations with her groom prior to her wedding. She must abstain from physical contact five days before she does the *hefsek taharah*.

What Is the Right Time of Day for the Hefsek Taharah Bedikah?

The *hefsek taharah bedikah* must be made before sunset.[5] The proper time is between a half-hour to one hour before sunset. If that time is inconvenient, the procedure may be carried out up to two hours prior to sunset.

(As long as the *bedikah* is carried out before sunset, it is acceptable. However, it is advisable to begin some time beforehand so that there will not be a nervous race against the clock. Also, should blood be discovered during the initial attempt at carrying out a *bedikah*, further attempts will be possible if sufficient time is available.)

In cases of extreme difficulty, for example, when the woman knows she'll be in a place where she will not be able to do a *hefsek taharah* before sunset (e.g., traveling on a bus), the woman should consult a Rav. (There are leniencies concerning doing a *hefsek taharah bedikah* earlier, but it is necessary to follow authoritative instructions.)

What Is the Procedure for the Hefsek Taharah?

1. Washing
2. The *Bedikah* — internal inspection with a *bedikah* cloth
3. The *Moch Dachuk*

1. Washing

A woman should wash the lower part of her body, or at least the genital area and inside the vagina, with water (warm water is suggested for her comfort). This washing is intended

---

5. A perpetual sunset calendar for various places around the world is available from Jewish Marriage Education (see last page of book).

to rinse out tiny spots of blood or residue from this area and help avoid the discovery of stains in the following days. When it is impossible for her to wash, it is sufficient for a woman to wipe herself internally instead.

On Shabbat and Yom Kippur, the procedure is changed slightly because of the Shabbat laws — and then a woman should use cold water or warm water which has been heated before Shabbat. Furthermore, she should not use a sponge or wet cloth but should wash herself only by hand. On Yom Kippur, Tishah B'Av, or during the week of her *shivah* mourning period, when washing for pleasure is prohibited, she may wash, but only the minimum area necessary.

It is advisable to wait ten to fifteen minutes after washing before performing the *bedikah* so that any excess water which might disturb the *bedikah* will drain, and the vagina's natural lubrication will return. This will ease the performing of the *bedikah*. If there is not sufficient time to wait these fifteen minutes, because it is close to sunset, a woman should wipe the inside of her vagina dry before performing the *bedikah*.[6]

2. The Bedikah

What Can Be Used for a Bedikah Cloth?

The *bedikah* cloth, which must be checked prior to use, must be absolutely clean, soft, white, absorbent, and made from a nonsynthetic fabric. Cotton cloth is generally used. It must be inspected before use. It is not permitted to use a tampon. It is not advisable to use cotton wool (cotton balls) since its strands separate. Do not use a big handkerchief because it may cause sores.

---

6. It is unnecessary and inadvisable to use a special douche for internal washing. Should a woman insist on doing so, she *must* wait at least fifteen minutes before making the *bedikah*.

The cloth should be between two-and-one-half to three inches square (six to eight centimeters square). Packages of personal cloths meeting these requirements can usually be obtained at a local *mikveh*, as well as from Jewish Marriage Education (see last page of book).

How Is the Bedikah, the Internal Inspection, Performed?

Wrap the cloth around the index finger. Be careful with a long fingernail, which may cause scratching. A suggested position for maximum comfort and efficiency is to lift one leg up on a chair.

Insert the finger with the cloth wrapped around it into the vagina as deep as possible. The entire finger should be inserted, slowly and gently. Rotate the finger inside the vagina to check all folds and clefts. Continue rotating the finger, as you direct it from deep inside back out while gently pressing on the vaginal canal.

This is intended to detect any drop of blood that may be left in the many folds of the vaginal lining. Rotating with a soft cloth is most efficient for this inspection. A tampon, by contrast, does not reach all the crevices.

If a woman finds difficulty in carrying out the *bedikah* due to dryness in the vagina, she may wet the cloth and then squeeze it out entirely before performing the *bedikah*. If she still has a problem, she should consult a Rav. Needless to say, a virgin bride should be careful to insert her finger only as far as is comfortable so as to avoid causing herself pain or any kind of sore.

It must be emphasized that this internal inspection is not merely a stringency but, rather, an absolute requirement for making a *hefsek taharah*. A woman who merely wipes herself externally has not fulfilled the law and cannot continue the *taharah* process until she performs this internal examination as prescribed.

Inspecting the Bedikah Cloth

Check the *bedikah* cloth by daylight (but not directly in the sun). It should be clean and free of any stains. If there is not enough light to check the cloth, place it in a clean place where it will not be lost and inspect it by daylight on the following day.

If stains are found on this *bedikah* cloth, one may wash again and carry out another inspection (with a different cloth) until a clean *bedikah* is obtained. This is on condition that there is still time before sunset. A woman inspecting herself a few times while trying to obtain a clean *hefsek taharah bedikah* should do so gently and carefully in order to prevent any irritation.

If questionable stains are still found on the cloth used for the last inspection before sunset, the cloth should be kept (for convenience, in an envelope), preferably after it is dry, to be taken later to a Rav. In the meantime, the woman should continue with the *taharah* process until the Rav's decision is made.

3. The Moch Dachuk

A widely-practiced custom, and one which must be adopted by every woman (unless she was instructed otherwise by a Rav) is the use of a *moch dachuk*.

What to Do

After the *hefsek taharah bedikah* has been made, insert another *bedikah* cloth (called a *moch dachuk*) into the vaginal canal and leave it there from before sunset until the emergence of three stars. At that time, the cloth should be removed and inspected. It should be kept overnight in a safe place (for example in an envelope), and rechecked again by daylight the next morning.

(In most packets of *bedikah* cloths, a few cloths made specifically for this purpose can be found. This is a regular *bedikah* cloth with a string attached to facilitate easy removal. But of course a regular *bedikah* cloth may be used.)

If a woman does not have any *bedikah* cloths left, she may use the cloth she used for the *hefsek taharah* for the *moch*, if it has first been thoroughly inspected and found clean.

The purpose of the *moch dachuk* is to ascertain that there is no further bleeding at the end of the day. Due to the woman's washing, the *hefsek taharah bedikah* may have been clean, but in fact the bleeding may not have completely ceased. The *moch* will detect this.

Suggestions Regarding the Moch Dachuk

1. Lie down if it is uncomfortable to walk around while the *moch* is in place.

2. If there was a question regarding the *hefsek taharah bedikah* and the time is nearing sunset, rotate the *moch* deeply in the vagina so it may also serve as a *hefsek taharah bedikah* if necessary.

3. It is not advisable to use a tampon as a *moch*, as it cannot be inspected as easily as a cloth.

4. Consult a Rav if inserting a *moch* causes staining as a result of irritation. (This may sometimes occur after childbirth.)

Additional Points

If the *hefsek taharah* or the *moch dachuk* inspections prove to be halachically unacceptable (e.g., stains, improper procedure, or inappropriate timing, etc.), the process should be attempted again on the following day before sunset.

Clean white underpants should be worn after the *hefsek taharah bedikah* and for the duration of the seven spotless days.

It is advisable for a woman to note the day she completed a halachically acceptable *hefsek taharah* on her personal calendar, in order to prevent mistakes.

The Seven Spotless Days — Shivah Neki'im

From the day after the *hefsek taharah*, a woman must count seven consecutive spotless days before immersing herself in the *mikveh*. She must inspect herself internally twice on each of these days, once in the morning after sunrise and once in the afternoon before sunset, to make sure that there is no sign of uterine bleeding.

How to Count

The seven days must be continuous and complete. For example: A woman making her *hefsek taharah* on Thursday before sunset begins her seven spotless days on Friday. She will immerse in the *mikveh* on the following Thursday night. In other words, *ohr le*, the beginning of, Friday (for a futher explanation of *ohr le*, see chapter 10).

The obligation to count these seven days stems from the verse: "And she shall count to herself seven days" (*Vayikra* 15:28). The verse implies that a woman should consciously count the days and not "remove her awareness" from the count. She should constantly know which of the seven days she is on.

The Torah regards a woman's intention and awareness as an integral part of the observance of this mitzvah. Thus, questions may arise if a woman makes a mental decision to interrupt her counting and stops paying attention to the count. She must ask a Rav if she subsequently wishes to resume her count where she left off. Take, for example, a woman who finds a stain which appears to her as blood, but which she sends to a Rav for clarification. Before receiving the Rav's answer she decides on her own that the stain is *tamei*, impure, therefore she discontinues her counting. Subsequently, the stain is shown to the Rav, who decides that it is *tahor*, pure and not problematic. This woman cannot simply resume her original counting where she left off, because she has, in halachic terms, "removed her awareness" from the counting. Rather, she must consult a Rav.

Another example of this concept: A woman interrupts her count of seven spotless days because her husband intends to travel out of town and not be back at the time of her scheduled immersion. In the meantime, his plans change, and he does not travel. Naturally the woman now wants to resume her original count, but she must consult a Rav to see if she may do so, or whether she must begin to count seven spotless days anew.

In order to avoid such problems, it is best that a woman should never interrupt her original counting. If a woman consults a Rav with a question regarding a stain in the seven spotless days, she should continue her counting while awaiting his answer.[7]

If a woman completes the seven-day count and must, because of a sound halachic reason, postpone her immersion, her counting is still valid and she may immerse when ready. How-

---

7. A situation may arise where the Rav's decision is delayed so that the woman does not know if she needs to start the count anew with a new *hefsek taharah* or if she should simply continue the seven-day count. In such a case, she may perform a new *hefsek taharah* "on condition," i.e., if the Rav's decision will be that she has to start the count anew, she has already done a new *hefsek taharah*. In this way, no days will be lost.

ever, white underpants and sheet need not be used for longer than the seven days.

What Must a Woman Do during the Seven Spotless Days?

1. The two *bedikot*, one in the morning after sunrise and one in the afternoon before sunset, are performed in the same manner as explained above regarding the *hefsek taharah bedikah* — insert the *bedikah* cloth deeply and rotate finger inside.

2. The vaginal area should not be washed before making the *bedikah*.

3. The *moch dachuk* procedure is not performed.

4. Women should wear white underpants, which should be inspected every day.

5. Throughout the ages, women have adopted, as a *minhag Yisrael*, the custom of sleeping on a clean white sheet, which should be inspected every day during these seven days.

Stains Found on a Bedikah Cloth or Other Stains (on the Body or Clothes) Discovered during These Seven Days

Consult a Rav and inform him:

1. when the *hefsek taharah bedikah* was done;

2. on which of the seven days the stain was found.

If the Rav decides that such a stain is a problematic one (in other words, it is not *tahor*), the woman must perform a new *hefsek taharah*, including the *moch dachuk* procedure, as soon as she is able and begin counting anew. In this instance, she need not wait five days before performing the *hefsek taharah* since such an interval had already passed before she began her first seven-day count.

What If the Bedikot Were Not Carried Out?

If a woman was unable or forgot to make *bedikot*, some leniency does apply. The basic rule is: one *bedikah* on the first day (following the day she made the *hefsek taharah*) and one *bedikah* on the seventh day, are imperative. If the *bedikot* were not carried out on any of the intermediate days, this does not invalidate a woman's seven-day count. Nevertheless, a woman must seriously try to do all fourteen *bedikot*. In all cases of missed *bedikot*, it is preferable to consult a Rav.

Suggestions and Advice

1. Make the morning *bedikah* immediately upon rising (after sunrise) so as not to forget.

2. If leaving home in the afternoon, take a packet of *bedikah* cloths with you, just in case you don't get home before sunset.

3. Consult a Rav if the *bedikot* cause discomfort of any sort.

4. Do not bathe immediately prior to doing a *bedikah*.

Chapter 6

Making the Heart Grow Fonder

RABBI ARYEH LEVIN, of blessed memory, was a renowned figure in Jerusalem. Those who knew him said that his entire being radiated true love and selfless concern for his fellow Jew.

Once, Reb Aryeh accompanied his wife on a visit to the doctor. The doctor was surprised when the couple entered his office together. Surely this woman was capable of consulting a physician on her own. But he was soon provided with an explanation. Reb Aryeh sat his wife comfortably in a chair and, turning to the doctor, said:

"Good morning, sir. We've come to seek your professional advice. You see, my wife's leg hurts us..."

The Torah wishes us to develop such empathetic marriages. But how can such a bond be established, and how can we preserve that bond over an entire lifetime? Human nature tends to tire of familiar situations. Indeed, one of the major factors behind today's skyrocketing divorce figures is downright boredom — a husband and wife simply lose interest in one another.

This is not solely a modern-day phenomenon. Thousands of years ago, the Torah recognized the problem and offered our people a basic guideline on how to overcome it:

> Rabbi Meir said: "Why did the Torah require a niddah to be impure for seven days? Because her husband could become bored with her and tire of her. Therefore, the Torah declares, 'Let her be ritually impure for seven days so that she will be as dear to her husband as when she entered the marriage canopy.' "
>
> (Niddah 31b)

While a woman is a *niddah*, she and her husband abstain from all touch, and, to paraphrase a popular expression, abstinence makes the heart grow fonder. The rules of the *harchakot*, maintaining a distance, are the framework in which a husband and wife practice their abstinence and through which it is hoped they will develop an even closer connection.

Many psychologists and marriage counselors adopt a similar approach when guiding a couple who are undergoing difficulties in their relationship. They suggest the couple avoid intimate relations for a set time in the hope that this separation will rekindle the natural bond between them.

There is, however, an obvious advantage when it is the Torah, rather than a psychologist or counselor, mandating the separation. When the reason for the separation is that G-d commands so, their feelings for each other grow. In contrast, when a separation is imposed by man, feelings of rejection and estrangement may arise.

The Torah's approach emphasizes that the separation between the couple is only temporary, and despite it being beneficial and necessary, it must not be viewed as an end in itself.

RIVKA, A WOMAN *in her late thirties, appreciates the logic be-*

hind the theory of the harchakot. She explains:

"*My husband and I have been married for twelve years and both feel we have a good, viable marriage, but there's always room for improvement. Almost by chance, we found out about the laws of Taharat HaMishpachah. We are open-minded individuals and, though we do not follow a strictly committed lifestyle, we were curious enough to try.*

"*Besides, society doesn't seem to offer any other reasonable, workable options to combat the possibility of a marriage going sour.*

"*We studied the subject and began following the laws. I must admit we did not really expect any serious changes. After all, we were basically satisfied with our relationship. Yet, enrichment came. Every visit to the mikveh gave us a sense of renewal and a chance to recapture the wedding joy.*

"*In addition,*" *adds Rivka,* "*for the first time in years, my husband went back to his old custom of calling me from work. It seems to happen precisely during the time when the laws of the harchakot apply! I sense that his desire to reach out to me is a by-product of the rules of the harchakot.*"

Rivka and her husband discovered how keeping the *harchakot* can help build communication between a couple by necessitating a different mode of interaction during this time. A husband and wife are forced to demonstrate their feelings for each other only through the acts of care and regard that are permitted by the halachah.

One of the *sheva berachot*, the wedding blessings, wishes a new couple "mirth, glad song, pleasure, and delight; love, brotherhood, peace, and companionship." The great mystic sage, the Maharal of Prague, explained the two clauses of the blessing as follows: the first clause, "mirth, glad song, pleasure, and delight," applies when a woman is *tehorah*; the second, "love, brotherhood, peace, and companionship," when she is a *niddah*. We see, then, that keeping the rules of *Taharat HaMishpachah* can endow a marriage with all possible forms of happiness.

The success of a marriage revolves around these two poles of *taharah* and *niddah*. The separation of the *niddah* period teaches a couple to develop a bond of friendship and harmony which finds expression in the dynamic and active happiness a couple experience when the woman is *tehorah*.

Indeed, the Torah desires that a man and a woman not behave with asceticism or abstinence. Nevertheless, our marriages can benefit greatly when, for a limited time, there is no intimate relationship. In this short span of time, different qualities, dimensions, and aspects of a relationship which otherwise may never develop have an opportunity to flower. We then find other means of expressing admiration and importance.

GAD AND CHEDVA are a couple who are, unfortunately, going through a difficult time in their marriage. They complain of disinterest and friction in their relationship.

Chedva confided in her longtime friend Esther and sought her advice. Esther invited them over to spend the weekend, hoping the calm Shabbat atmosphere would be conducive to productive communication. Perhaps she and her husband would be able to help them solve a few of their difficulties.

On Friday afternoon, Gad and Chedva arrived with their four-year-old daughter, Chanie. Throughout Shabbat, Esther noticed that the couple showered affection on one another in a very obvious manner.

When Esther and Chedva began talking about Chedva's mar-

riage, Esther mentioned her observation to her friend. With an uneasy, apologetic look on her face, Chedva explained, "Esther, I want you to understand that though Gad and I are having problems, we haven't entirely given up on our marriage. And all the while we believe our problems are solvable, we really want Chanie to think that Mommy and Daddy appreciate each other."

"What a shame," Esther thought to herself. "That poor Chanie needs to believe that her parents respect and appreciate one another only from the artificial show of physical affection."

There are many ways to communicate regard for one's spouse. How easy it is to forget that listening attentively and respectfully to one another, or simply sharing each other's company, works to strengthen the bond between man and wife. Following the rules of the *harchakot* forces the couple to devote more time to these subtler forms of interpersonal communication.

The relationship which is built in a couple's younger years will still be strong in later years, when the physical bond is not identical to what it was in the early years of marriage. The positive influence which results from the observance of the *harchakot* will remain even years later, when they are not applicable any longer (because the wife has passed menopause).

It must be emphasized that the *harchakot* are not only an end in themselves, to distance the couple from that which is forbidden, but they are also a means for developing a relationship between the couple.

On the other hand, when the woman is *tehorah*, and thus other ways for developing their relationship are available, the *harchakot* are not practiced. A woman who is *tehorah* for a long period of time (for example, when pregnant or nursing) need not fear that the quality of her marriage will suffer because she does not have opportunity to practice the *harchakot*.

The Torah wants a man and woman to express whichever type of bond is required for each couple — the one dictated when a woman is a *niddah*, the other when she is *tehorah*. Our task is to derive the maximum benefit from the possibilities offered by both types of situations.

JONATHAN AND MICHAL are a young couple who recently became committed to following the laws of Taharat HaMishpachah. The system as a whole appealed to them, and they considered it a worthwhile "investment" in their marriage, family, and Jewish identity. Only one chapter of the laws Michal found difficult to accept — the harchakot.

"Look, we're doing the main things," she explained. "That's fine for me, and I think it's enough!"

Little did Michal know how far from "fine" this was for her husband and how much this endangered their new road. Unwilling to rock the boat, as they were both quite new at this, he held his peace. But it all came out in the open quite unexpectedly one evening.

They were eating dinner with the Rabbi and his wife. Having been the ones to introduce the couple to the subject of Taharat HaMishpachah, the Rabbi and Rebbetzin inquired as to how they were managing with their new lifestyle.

Michal hesitated for a moment, then admitted with sincerity, "Well, we don't really keep the details of the harchakot."

Jonathan shifted uneasily in his chair. "Actually, Rabbi, I honestly think that total observance of the laws would be better, but..."

Michal stared at her husband unbelievingly — had she been that insensitive? On the way home, Michal and her husband finally spoke about the issue. It was only then that she realized how difficult it was for him to keep the laws that they both so wanted to keep, simply because she ignored the existence of some of them she thought were marginal.

The *harchakot* relate very closely to the physical nature of both a husband and a wife. Men and women are different, and the Torah's rules provide an opportunity for both to become more aware of the other's natural makeup.

The *harchakot* teach a woman to forego some of her own demands for closeness from her husband in order to distance them both from the serious prohibition of *niddah* at this time. They also protect the woman and allow for a welcome opportunity for privacy, which she perhaps naturally desires for various reasons, among them physical discomfort, hormonal changes, and general moodiness. One English researcher, Dr. White, writes, "At this time, women are psychologically and emotionally depressed as a result of their hormonal changes. It is inadvisable for them to engage in marital relations with their husbands at this time." If not for the Torah laws which obligate him, a husband might feel slighted and regard his wife's desire for privacy as a personal insult.

A man who observes the *harchakot* does not view his wife's behavior as a disinterest in himself. The *harchakot* guarantee a woman's rights to privacy while preserving a spirit of peace and harmony within the home.

For precisely this reason, many non-Jewish observers have paid tribute to the Jewish laws of *Taharat HaMishpachah*. Dr. Marie C. Stopes, an English physician who has done extensive research in the area of the relations between couples, explains:

"I have heard about the Jewish marital laws of Family Purity. They depict the most advanced lifestyle in the world today, being in total harmony with the functioning of a woman's body. The requirement for abstinence after menstruation and the time for resuming relations correspond precisely to a woman's natural tides. Couples who adhere to these laws are sure to enjoy a happy marriage."

The practical observance of the *harchakot* demands effort and entails withstanding challenges which are not always easy. Indeed, the laws of the *harchakot* teach us self-control. Our Sages teach (*Avot* 4:1), "Who is strong? He who subdues his personal inclination, as it is said, 'He who is slow to anger is better than the strong man, and a master of his passions is better than a conqueror of a city.' " The Torah does not demand that man abolish his drives completely but rather that he take the golden path, subduing his urges, controlling them, knowing how to direct them in the correct time, the correct place, and the correct manner. Only the halachah itself can determine for us what is this golden path. It is the halachah which determines the laws of *Taharat HaMishpachah* in general and the laws of the *harchakot* in particular. Following these ensures us control over our drives, so that we do not become slaves to passion.

It must be emphasized that all the advantages mentioned that result from observing the *harchakot* are not the reason for keeping them. There is only one reason for observing the *harchakot*: to fulfill G-d's will. As a by-product of the fulfillment of G-d's will, we can derive the above and other benefits.

In fact, the main purpose in keeping the *harchakot* is to serve as a constant reminder of the wife's *niddah* state and the separation that it requires. Adherence to these rules prevents a person from transgressing Torah prohibitions during the *niddah* period.

It is important to know that these rules were commanded by G-d. Therefore, even though at times we might think that certain rules are too strict and others too lenient, we with our human logic are not able to comprehend them. Our faith in the Creator who created us and knows what is good for us makes it easier for us to keep Torah and mitzvot whether we understand them or not.

TAMMY IS A YOUNG WOMAN who came across a pamphlet on Taharat HaMishpachah. It piqued her curiosity, and she attended the series of lectures offered in the pamphlet. When the topic of harchakot was introduced, Tammy was impressed. Nevertheless, she had one basic question.

"Excuse me," she said as she raised her hand. "I'm not quite sure these rules can be accepted so universally. After all, we are dealing with a very personal subject. Take, for example, one of the laws you just described. You said that a couple mustn't simultaneously sip a drink from the same bottle when the woman is a niddah even if using separate straws. But, surely, human natures vary. For one couple, that may be an act of closeness. However, another might feel very uncomfortable doing that very same thing. Who is to say what arouses a heartfelt bond between a couple?"

"True," nodded the lecturer. "People's feelings vary. Indeed, what will constitute an expression of closeness today might evoke a totally indifferent reaction tomorrow. There's no way that human logic could produce these rules. Knowing that fact is a key to understanding and appreciating these laws. Man didn't make them. G-d did. It is simple and obvious that the Creator knows His creation. Indeed, He knows us better than we know ourselves.

"At times, a particular situation described by the harchakot may not appear logical, but we must understand that the Torah's laws address themselves to the people as a whole, and individual circumstances have to be considered within this larger context.

"Besides," the lecturer concluded with a smile, "the Torah encourages an intensity of feeling between husband and wife, and

such a high level of sensitivity, that they are observing the commandment to 'love one another as oneself' to its maximum, and every gesture should count."

Despite all the advantages the *harchakot* can bring us, there is a natural tendency to think they are restrictive. Indeed, there are many who view them as cumbersome burdens. A woman who has such feelings must be willing to accept and carry out G-d's will despite her own discomfort. However, she must also remember what our Sages teach us: "The reward is in proportion to the effort" (*Avot* 5:23). In other words, her reward is in accordance with the difficulty she had in observing the law. A woman is in fact promised great reward for the observance of the *harchakot*.

If you are very careful during the seven days of niddah...you will merit children who are good, friendly, and unique within their generation. Every woman who behaves with purity and is careful when she is a niddah and with her immersion...merits righteous children.

(Ohr Zarua)

We are told that at the time of Creation, after the delicate little dove was brought into being, it confronted its Creator with a complaint: "G-d, why did You create me so fragile and small? My coloring is white, easily spotted by all animals of prey. I can hardly escape my pursuers."

G-d accepted the complaint and gently attached a pair of wings to the dove's vulnerable body.

On the following day, the dove returned with a further grievance. "G-d, now it's even worse than before. Yesterday, it wasn't easy to run away from the predators, but still, all I had was my own body to carry. Now I also have to pull along these two burdensome wings you gave me."

G-d smiled upon the little dove, and patiently taught her how to use those wings and fly. The dove learned quickly to make use of G-d's gift and was soon flying, soaring to the clouds.

The *harchakot* and, for that matter, the totality of Torah and mitzvot may occasionally appear as burdens. However, that is only because of the limited nature of our perception and our lack of knowledge of how to grow from the mitzvot. If we apply ourselves and study G-d's commandments we will be able to appreciate them and use them as a means to elevate ourselves and, consequently, our marriages.

One may think that since during this period of time the physical dimension of marriage is missing, there will be increased conflict. But if both husband and wife are sensitive and creative the utmost peace may be maintained. A midrash in *Otzar HaMidrashim* tells us how conflict was avoided in the home of Mefiboshet, the son of King Shaul. Whenever there was a conflict in the home, Mefiboshet's aide, Tziba, would lay the table in order to have the conflicting parties partake in a festive meal, even adding wine, if necessary, to make them happy. Heaven rewarded him greatly for his ability to avoid disputes in his master's home. With a little creativity one can maintain peace at any time or any place.

Chapter 7

Keeping a Distance

The Laws of the Harchakot

> *And thou shalt not approach unto a woman to uncover her*
> *nakedness as long as she is impure by her uncleanness.*
>
> *(Vayikra 18:19)*

WITH THIS VERSE, the Torah prohibits not only marital relations, but all forms of physical closeness between husband and wife from the time a woman enters the *niddah* state until after her immersion in a *mikveh*. During this time, the couple must observe the set of rules referred to as the *harchakot*.

Our Sages describe these rules as a "hedge of roses" (*Sanhedrin* 37a). They remind the couple of the woman's status and have been established for her protection. These laws assist a couple in preventing situations which could lead to forbidden physical closeness. All physical contact between man and wife while the woman is a *niddah* is a most serious transgression of Torah law.

The laws of the *harchakot* will guide a couple in how to behave in the wide variety of everyday situations they will encounter while the woman is a *niddah*. Unless specified otherwise, these rules apply equally to both husband and wife.

Touching

1. A husband and wife may not touch each other even indirectly, that is, using an intermediate object. (For example, brushing dirt off one another.)

2. They may not touch each other's clothes while they are being worn. (Thus, one cannot brush dust off the other's clothes.)

3. A couple may not hand objects, even long ones, to each other or handle an object at the same time. (In times of great necessity, there are leniencies regarding handing over a baby if he is old enough to show he wants to move to the other parent.)

4. They may not throw an object to each other, in any manner at all.

5. They may not sit together on a seat which moves when sat on (e.g., a rocking chair or swing) or on a sofa with one cushion, unless another person is sitting between them or an obvious object is placed there.

6. When traveling for pleasure (e.g., on vacation) in a car, they may not sit on an undivided seat. When there is no other possibility available they should place an obvious object between them, and preferably they should have other passengers with them.

7. When traveling for business or another necessary trip (e.g., to work), they may sit on the same seat, but they must be careful not to touch one another. (It is advisable

to place an obvious object between them.) If the seat does not move, as in a bus, they may share a double seat but they may not touch.

Eating

1. When eating at the same table, a husband and wife must make an obvious deviation from their norm. For example:

   a) setting an object which is not needed for that meal between their plates;

   b) or, the wife sitting in a different place than usual;

   c) or, using individual table mats for one or both of them;

   d) or, having an additional person(s) sit between them. In a time of necessity one may be lenient if there are others around the table even not between them.

2. A couple may not eat or drink from the same plate, dish, or cup (e.g., drinking from one soda can even with two straws is forbidden). Therefore, when food is served on a general serving dish, they should both take food onto their individual plates and not eat directly from the serving dish. However, they may help themselves directly to foods which are not taken frequently, e.g., bread, fruit, or cake may be taken directly from the serving dish.

   In contrast, foods commonly eaten from hand to mouth (e.g., nuts, dried fruit, or the like) must be placed on individual settings.

3. A husband may not eat or drink from his wife's leftovers in her presence, even if more food is added to the plate. If in the meantime someone else has eaten or drunk from her leftovers, or they have been transferred to another plate, or she has left the room, he may eat them.

4. If the husband does not know that the leftovers are his wife's, she is not obligated to tell him, and he may eat them.

5. A wife may eat or drink from her husband's leftovers.

6. A husband or wife may not serve food or pour drinks for each other unless they do so in a fashion which shows a deviation from their usual manner (e.g., serving with the left hand or setting down the plate slightly removed from the spouse's place).

7. A wife may pour wine for her husband only in a fashion which shows a deviation from her usual manner. But a husband may not pour wine for his wife. (There is no problem with a wife drinking from her husband's kiddush cup, as long as he places it on the table and does not direct it specifically to her.)

Bedroom Arrangements

1. The couple must sleep in separate beds. A double bed that does not separate into two cannot be used no matter how wide it is.

2. Space must be made between the two beds so that neither the beds nor the bedding touch. It is preferable to be stringent and have the distance between them an arms' length.

3. A husband may not sit or lie on his wife's bed, even if she is not present in the room, as long as she is in town.

4. A wife may not lie on her husband's bed in his presence, but she may sit on it. When he is not present, she may lie on it.

5. They may not prepare each other's bed for sleeping in each other's presence.

Washing and Bathing

1. A couple may not prepare water for each other to wash or bathe with (or even add water to the bathtub) in the other's presence. (They may prepare water for *negel vasser*, the required morning washing.)

Additional Restrictions

1. A husband and wife may not engage in behavior that is likely to arouse desire. (Obviously, this does not mean that during the time the woman is a *niddah*, she and her husband must appear grumpy and sour faced!) During this time, a woman should take care of her appearance so that she looks nice for her husband, but not provocative.

2. A husband may not see parts of his wife's body that are usually covered. Thus, a woman must not dress in front of her husband.

3. A husband may not intentionally smell his wife's perfume, whether it is on her or on her clothes.

4. A husband may not listen to his wife singing.

5. A couple should not discuss with each other subjects which are likely to arouse desire. Study and clarification of the *niddah* laws is permitted.

6. A couple must observe the *harchakot* even when one of them is sick and needs the care of the other. Nevertheless, when there is no one else to take care of the sick spouse, some contact is permitted, excluding acts of affection. Concerning washing and bed preparation there are different laws for the husband and for the wife. If the husband is sick — she is allowed to assist him to eat and

rise but she should try to avoid as much as possible washing him and preparing his bed. If the wife is sick — only at a time of great need may he assist her to eat and rise and only if absolutely necessary should he wash her, and he should try as far as possible not to actually touch her. In all cases it is preferable to ask a Rav.

Chapter 8

The Mysterious Waters

MRS. KLEIN AND her daughter, Rosa, were the only members of their family who, after much hardship, finally emigrated from behind the Iron Curtain. Mrs. Klein's husband had passed away in Russia, and their son, Joseph, was not granted an exit visa.

Weary but hopeful, the two women began a new life in Eretz Yisrael. Rosa attended high school and continued her studies in a teachers' seminary. Upon her engagement to a fine young man, Rosa found herself busy preparing for her wedding.

After one particularly tiring day of errands and shopping, Mrs. Klein and her daughter spent the evening relaxing in their living room. Mrs. Klein was in an expansive mood and began to reminisce about life in Russia.

"You know, Rosa," she said, "there is no way you can appreciate how happy your father would be to know that his daughter is getting married in Eretz Yisrael and preparing to live a life of Torah and mitzvot.

"You were a young girl when we still lived in Russia, and there were many secrets we were forced to keep from you. One of them was that, in our basement, we maintained a mikveh which

enabled forty Jewish families in our village to keep the laws of Taharat HaMishpachah.

"You cannot imagine the enormous effort and constant danger such a project involved. From the moment we started building, we had to hide our doings from the KGB. Your father built most of the mikveh himself. Nevertheless, how does one hide hundreds of kilograms of cement from nosy neighbors? And, of course, the mikveh had to be 100 percent kosher. Your father would have it no other way. He contacted a Rabbi from faraway Moscow and offered to pay his entire fare if he would come and guide him in the construction. At first, the Rabbi was reluctant. The penalty for such a crime, should they be detected, was certain death. But your father begged him and the Rabbi agreed."

"And the neighbors never found out?" asked Rosa in amazement.

"Well, we did have some close calls," replied her mother. "Once, a troublesome neighbor was determined to find out where the trapdoor at the bottom of the staircase led. He came upon your father just as he was changing the water.

" 'Hello, Mr. Klein! What is this?'

"Your father looked up, the calm expression on his face disclosing none of his inner fears. 'Oh, it's you, Gregory! As you know, we often have trouble with our water supply in this building. I got fed up and decided to construct my own private well. I didn't want anyone to find out, otherwise we'd be bombarded every time there is a shortage!'

"Gregory continued to eye him with obvious suspicion. Your father then scooped up a cupful of the water which forty families had used in the mikveh for almost a year. 'It's very tasty,' he continued, downing the whole cup. 'Can I offer you a drink?' Declining the offer, Gregory retreated, no longer curious. Your father followed after him: 'If you promise not to tell anyone, I'll

let you use this well when there's a shortage.' "

Rosa smiled at her father's ingenuity, but her face quickly turned serious: "Mother, how could you have lived with such constant fear?"

Mrs. Klein replied quietly: "How could we have lived otherwise?"

The concepts of *taharah*, ritual purity, and *tumah*, impurity, given us in the Torah transcend our comprehension. As the Rambam explains:

> *It is clear that the laws of ritual purity and impurity are decrees of the Torah that cannot be comprehended by human wisdom...*
>
> *(Hilchot Mikvaot 11:12)*

Because these concepts are spiritual in nature, the transition from the state of *tumah* (of being a *niddah*) to the state of *taharah* must by definition be a G-dly process. The culmination of this process involves preparation for and immersion in the *mikveh*. Acting on faith alone, Jewish families throughout the ages have been willing to put their lives on the line in order that women may immerse and lead lives of purity and devotion to G-d.

What Is a Mikveh?

The word *mikveh* literally means "gathering." In the Torah's discussion of the laws of ritual purity and impurity, it states, "Nevertheless, a fountain or a cistern wherein is a gathering of water shall be pure..." (*Vayikra* 11:36).

Based on this verse and other teachings, our Sages have articulated the detailed laws governing the construction of a *mikveh*, a pool containing this "gathering of water." Throughout the centuries, wherever Jews have lived, they have followed these laws and constructed *mikvaot*. So vital is this structure to the life of a Jewish community that Torah law requires its construction to precede the building of a synagogue or purchasing a Torah scroll.

Today, the *mikveh* is found within the confines of a building, and there are usually a number of *mikvaot* as well as bathing rooms and showers, and a waiting room. Some are quite elegant and luxurious and offer extras such as beauty salons, which add to the pleasure of the visit.

However, we must not let all these "extras" cause us to lose sight of the fundamentally spiritual nature of the *mikveh* experience. Going to the *mikveh* is essentially a process of spiritual transition to a state of spiritual purity. How far this idea is from the widespread misconception which links the term *tumah* to uncleanliness. It is spiritual impurity and not actual dirt which we remove with our immersions.

It is difficult to understand how such a misconception could have arisen, as it is mandatory to bathe very thoroughly

By courtesy of the Israel Center for Taharat HaMishpachah

before immersing in the *mikveh*, as explained in the laws detailed in the next chapter. Immersion in the *mikveh* is mentioned in the Torah on other occasions when cleanliness is not the issue. For example, before the giving of the Torah on Mount Sinai, the entire Jewish people were commanded to immerse in a *mikveh*. When the priests were initiated into service in the Temple, and as part of that service, they were frequently required to immerse in a *mikveh*. The High Priest himself was instructed to immerse in a *mikveh* five times on Yom Kippur. The process of conversion to Judaism requires immersion in a *mikveh*.

These examples give us a clearer picture of the idea behind the mitzvah: preparing a person to enter into a new spiritual status.

In all mitzvot, the form which the mitzvah is to take — how it is performed — and the result desired from its performance are inseparable. The only way we can attain the spiritual levels to which the Torah leads us is by using the specific tools which G-d has designed for this purpose. Would anyone suggest blowing a trumpet instead of a shofar on Rosh HaShanah?

Similarly, a *mikveh* is not a glorified bathtub, sauna, or swimming pool. Yes, cleanliness is important to the mitzvah of immersion, but only as a preparatory step. In no way can the bath in the bathtub, which is a precondition to immersion, take the place of immersion in the *mikveh*. The bathing is only the preparation for the immersion which causes the spiritual transformation. The Divinely ordained change of status from *tumah* to *taharah* must be carried out in the manner prescribed in the Torah — by immersion in the *mikveh*. The Rambam summarizes this issue: "Immersion from impurities is also one of the laws which must be accepted on faith...for ritual impurity is not mud or filth which washes off with water" (*Hilchot Mikvaot* 11:12).

RUTH IS A TAHARAT HAMISHPACHAH counselor who teaches women the subject on an individual basis. Rabbis often recommend her name to brides who need to learn the laws in preparation for their marriage. Often, Ruth accompanies "her" brides to the mikveh for their first time. On one such visit something quite unusual happened.

While the bride bathed before immersion, Ruth joined the mother, who was also accompanying her daughter, in the waiting room.

"You know," the mother said as they were waiting, "my daughter has been sharing with me her learning experience with you. I'm really quite impressed with some of your ideas."

"They're not my ideas," smiled Ruth. "They're the Torah's. I'm just trained to explain them to others. As a matter of fact, not long ago, the passing on of this heritage was strictly a mother-daughter affair."

"Yes, I know," nodded the mother. "My mother taught me the laws of Taharat HaMishpachah and I still follow some of them."

Ruth looked at the woman in surprise. She knew the bride's family was "traditional," but that was a far cry from observing the mitzvot.

The mother continued: "I separate from my husband for the required amount of time. I count the days and even do the personal inspections. It's only the mikveh I leave out. I just take a bath at the end of the seven days. You see, I feel the requirement to immerse in a mikveh unnecessary when we live in such a modern world, where sanitary conditions are of such a high standard."

Ruth had heard this argument before. She was about to answer and explain when, suddenly, the woman continued: "Isn't it strange — tonight is the right time for me to take my bath."

Ruth immediately perked up. What remarkable Divine intervention has worked things this way! Forget the rational discus-

sions and arguments! This woman is going to immerse in the mikveh tonight, she decided.

It did not take too much convincing. The mother herself was inspired by the extraordinary turn of events. A short while later, she entered the bathing room, received basic instruction, and, for the first time in her life, the woman immersed in a mikveh. On her way home that night, Ruth mused to herself: "What a strange generation we are living in. Like daughter, like mother..."

The lesson Ruth taught the bride's mother is clearly expressed by the Rambam:

> *If she washed in a bath, even if all the waters in the world fell over her, she remains in precisely the same condition as before bathing...as nothing changes the status from impure to pure except the immersion in a mikveh.*
>
> (Hilchot Issurei Biah 11:16)

Her whole married life, this woman, in her innocence, had thought that these laws did not obligate her because she did not understand the reason for them. Indeed, it is only the strength of faith which enables us to accept the principles of ritual impurity, purity, and immersion. Nevertheless, a thorough examination of these laws will reveal a number of profound philosophical insights which add to our understanding of the issue. Jewish philosophy and mysticism have devoted much thought to discovering these insights.

Many laws pertaining to impurity, *tumah*, revolve around the absence of life. For example, contact with a human corpse or the carcass of an animal renders a Jew impure, *tamei*.

When a woman begins to menstruate, she, too, experiences a loss of potential life. A month has gone by in which the egg readied for conception has gone unused. The Torah considers this loss of potential life a source of *tumah*.

In contrast, water is the source of all life. All living entities require water for their survival. An embryo, too, develops enclosed in a sac of water.

The Divine commandment of immersion in a *mikveh* can be seen as a transition from death and loss to the renewal of life. Beneath the *mikveh*'s waters, a woman rejuvenates herself spiritually. This allows her to once again become a potential partner with G-d and her husband in the act of creation. She emerges from the life-giving waters "born anew" and ready to conceive anew.

> *Each and every month, a woman renews herself by immersing in the mikveh and returns to her husband, and she is as dear to him as on the day of the wedding. Just as the moon renews itself each Rosh Chodesh, and all await to see it, so a woman when she becomes renewed each month, her husband awaits her and she is dear to him like a new wife.*
>
> (Pirkei DeRabbi Eliezer, Ohr Zarua 452)

"I REMEMBER," RECALLS CHAVA, "the first time I had to go to the mikveh. The whole idea seemed strange and foreign to me. But I had no choice about the matter. My fiancé insisted that I go at least the one time before our wedding.

"I was determined to make it a quick dip and get out of there as soon as possible! Strangely enough, I found myself enjoying every moment. As I descended the steps and slowly immersed in the water, a sense of rejuvenation overtook me.

"I was overwhelmed by the experience and needed to express my new feelings. As if reading my thoughts, the attendant presented me with a lovely prayer inscribed on a card.

"There I was, sitting on the couch in the waiting room reading the prayer, when I heard a familiar honk from outside. I thanked the attendant and hurried outside. My mother was waiting in the car.

" 'What took you so long?' she asked. 'You said it would take only a minute.'

" 'I don't know, Ma. I was convinced this would be my first and last time, but somehow I got "immersed" in the mikveh experience. I have a feeling this won't be my last time either.' "

As stated earlier, it is not just any water that is capable of bringing about the transition from *tumah* to *taharah*. A bath, shower, or another type of pool cannot serve as a *mikveh*. What is so unique about the *mikveh's* waters?

Many of us think "water is water." However, any tourist knows that the quality and taste of water in the country he is visiting is not the same as the water back home. Scientists have discovered a tangible physical difference between soft water and heavy water. Is it so far-fetched to comprehend differences between the spiritual nature of one body of water and that of another? He who commanded the *mikveh* waters to purify did not command so concerning tap water.

The laws concerning the erection of a kosher *mikveh* provide an insight into the spiritual nature of the *mikveh's* waters. The *mikveh* in which we immerse ourselves is filled with fresh tap water but connected to it is a cistern containing rain or well water. Thus the water in which we immerse is connected to water that comes directly from a natural source.

Why must a woman immerse specifically in waters which come straight from their natural source?

The connection to these natural waters alludes to a connection with the primeval waters of creation. The spiritual message of such an association is obvious.

Parashat Bereishit tells of the creation of Adam, the first man, whom G-d placed in the Garden of Eden and to whom He gave one commandment only: not to eat from the Tree of

Knowledge. Further it tells of the serpent who persuades Chava to disobey G-d's commandment; as a result Adam is banished from the Garden. In the middle of the story, and seemingly disconnected to the narration, the Torah tells us (2:10): "And a river went out of Eden to water the Garden and from thence it was parted and became four heads." The commentators ask: What is the message and the significance of the river which went out of the Garden?

The first man was created to dwell in the Garden of Eden, and his being there showed his perfection. He was taken out of the Garden only after he sinned, thereby blemishing his perfection. Since the sin of the first man, the whole of humanity is shut out of the Garden of Eden, a fact which indicates its imperfection. There is only one connection between the world out of the Garden of Eden — the imperfect world — and the world within the Garden — the world of perfection. This is the river which goes out from Eden, which connects and joins the world of perfection with the world of imperfection.

The *Tikunei Zohar* points out that the Hebrew letters making up the word *mikveh* are the same letters which make up the word *kumah*, "to rise." By immersing in the *mikveh*, which is a concentration of water coming directly from its natural source — and as we know all the waters of the world are connected (therefore the *mikveh* waters are connected with the waters of the river which comes out of Gan Eden) — man rises and leaves his state of imperfection and connects to a situation of perfection.

Now the words of our great Sage are clear:

> *Shammai said: "Great is the woman who observes the laws of niddah. They separate her from sin and bring her close to Gan Eden."*
>
> (Breita Niddah 81a)

The Dvar Avraham quotes world-renowned scientists who proved that rain water is more beneficial to agriculture than man-made irrigation systems, because the water that comes directly from heaven leaves the potash and other G-d-given treasures in the ground, while man-made irrigation systems wash away from the ground many important substances. In this way he explains the verse, "When rain falls and snow from heaven and it gives birth and makes grow..." (*Yishayahu* 55:10). It is clear that there is a difference between water which comes directly from Heaven without being touched by man versus all other waters.

RABBI SHUSTER IS THE LEADER of a Jewish community in Southern California. After many months of determined effort, a beautiful mikveh building was dedicated in the posh suburban neighborhood, which until now had no mikveh at all. Many a synagogue member was skeptical as to the extent of its planned use and popularity.

Rabbi Shuster looked at the matter from a different perspective. He had given many lectures, classes, and workshops discussing the topic of Taharat HaMishpachah. He felt that an attractive, modern mikveh would boost the practical application of the theoretical principles he had been teaching.

Despite the many obstacles he had to overcome, all went well for the good Rabbi except for...the weather! The expected rain had not fallen, and the mikveh could not be filled. In Southern California, heavy rains fall only a few months a year, so it seemed as if there was no choice but to wait for the next rainy season.

But Rabbi Shuster was not to be discouraged. He would not take "wait" for an answer when it came to the observance of mitzvot! "Is there no other alternative?" he asked a prominent halachic authority.

After investigating the matter in depth, they arrived at a pos-
sible solution. There is a mishnah (Tractate Mikvaot 7:1) which
teaches that a mikveh can be started from snow. As long as it does
not melt before it is placed in the mikveh, it is considered "natural
water" and may be used. There was plenty of snow atop the peaks
of the Sierras! Cases of fresh snow could be packed and shipped
down south in refrigerated trucks.

What a sight to behold! Two bearded gentlemen, black hats on
their heads and with the distinguished look of the Rabbinate
about them, were standing atop a mountain peak in large rubber
boots, packing snow into wire carriers. The truck drivers had
quite a story to tell when they returned.

Little did the women who used the mikveh back home know
that what enabled them to enjoy a warm, comfortable immersion
was a snowy mountaintop a hundred miles away.

A fundamental tenet of Judaism is the sanctification of time. Men achieve this sanctification through performance of the time-bound mitzvot. Women, however, are freed of the requirement to perform the positive time-bound mitzvot. The holiness which the man acquires through the performance of the time-bound mitzvot is achieved by the woman through immersion, which is performed within a specific time cycle.

Our Sages have greatly stressed the requirement to immerse in the *mikveh* "on time," at the end of the seven spotless days. They have elaborated on the immense merit and reward deserved by a woman who sanctifies time by immersing on time. Rav Yitzchak Luria, the Saintly Ari, declared that from time to time souls with great spiritual potentials are drawn down to this world. Who merits to conceive them? Women who immerse on time and keep the mitzvah of *onah*, the union between husband and wife.

ONE LATE WINTER NIGHT, the telephone rang in the home of Mrs. Jacobs, a Taharat HaMishpachah counselor. It was Tali.

"Oh, Mrs. Jacobs!" she cried in exasperation. "Everything seems to have gone wrong for me today. Tonight is my time to immerse in the mikveh, but I just can't make it. My refrigerator broke down, and I spent hours trying to get a repair man. I finally decided to go out to the company myself but got stuck in a traffic jam. Then my in-laws arrived for a supper that wasn't cooked...

"My head is spinning. I remember you teaching me that a woman should not postpone her immersion, but couldn't this time be an exception? I'm not in the mood. Besides by now the mikveh is probably locked, and it's snowing outside. I just can't handle anything else tonight!"

The counselor calmed her and reminded her of the importance of immersing on time. Her gentle tone and relaxed response helped Tali regain her equilibrium. Yet, it didn't seem possible. "But it's too late now, and I haven't even prepared myself," argued Tali.

Mrs. Jacobs assured her that it would be okay. "I'll call the mikveh attendant and make a special request. We won't even trouble her to come down. I have a key. I'll take you myself and supervise you as required."

"But it's 10:30 at night."

The counselor was not to be dissuaded. "Give me a ring when you're ready. I'll be waiting by my door."

Tali could not believe this woman's devotion. How could she refuse her generous offer? Few other people ventured out that snowy night, but Tali was one of them.

Later that night, Tali could not help feeling pleased with herself. She had gone to the mikveh on time despite the odds against her. She had even more reason to be pleased when she gave birth to her first daughter exactly nine months later, after seven childless years of marriage.

Immersion in the *mikveh* differs from all other mitzvot in one crucial way. All other mitzvot involve the usage of one or a few parts of the body. Tefillin are placed on the arm and head; matzo is eaten with the mouth, etc. By contrast, as a women descends into the waters of the *mikveh*, she is entirely "immersed" in the fulfillment of a mitzvah.

This principle is reflected in the laws requiring us to remove from the body any kind of *chatzitzah*, intervening object, which may prevent complete contact with the water. Nothing must stand between the woman and the water that enables her to change her status from *tumah* to *taharah*. As the Rambam states:

> *A woman cannot emerge from the state of impurity...until she immerses in the waters of a kosher mikveh without having anything intervening between her flesh and the water.*
> (Hilchot Issurei Biah 11:16)

A very deep point is indicated here. Immersion in the *mikveh* represents a covenant with the source of all existence, G-d. A woman who immerses so that her entire body is covered by the waters of the *mikveh* is connecting totally, with her entire being, to G-d. It is only after such a total bonding that one can become purified.

WHEN LEAH, MRS. GOLD'S daughter, was about to be married, she could not understand why her mother was making such a fuss over the choice of a Taharat HaMishpachah teacher. The laws were the laws, weren't they?

"The laws are the laws," Mrs. Gold admitted. Though the problem is sometimes with the pupil, she thought, as she sadly recalled how she had learned these laws without paying too much attention to them and how she had never realized the importance of having a mikveh attendant present upon immersion. For two

long years she had immersed without an attendant present. The worst part was that, since she didn't like the water, she had only immersed up to her chin. What heartache she had undergone when she discovered she had not fulfilled her obligation to immerse and had remained a niddah for all that time.

The laws of *Taharat HaMishpachah* are highly detailed, and a woman who is not confident in her knowledge might grow fearful or nervous in her observance. For this reason the laws must be studied with a teacher who has learnt to teach the subject clearly and simply. A student who observes this mitzvah confidently and with the knowledge that without a doubt she has kept every detail of the law experiences great joy. As it says, "There is no joy greater than that of the resolving of doubts."

G-d is described as *Mikveh Yisrael*, literally, "the Hope of Israel" (*Yirmeyahu* 17:13). The Metzudot explains, "Therefore it is correct that the hope of Israel should be in G-d." Rabbi Akiva explains the connection, "Fortunate are you O Israel... See who purifies you — your Father in Heaven! As it states, 'I throw on you pure water and you become pure,' and 'G-d is the *mikveh* of Israel.' Just as the *mikveh* purifies the impure, so G-d purifies Israel" (*Yoma* 85).

The Torah concepts are interrelated: When Israel appreciates that it is G-d who purifies them, they can face the future with true hope and trust. A woman who immerses in the *mikveh* recognizes that it is G-d who purifies, so she too can look forward to the future, full of hope and trust.

Suggested Prayer before Immersion[1]

Master of the world: With an inspired heart, I approach the fulfillment of the mitzvah of immersion for the sake of purity. I have made an effort to be faithful to Your mitzvot and I look forward to Your salvation. Just as the *mikveh*'s waters purify me spiritually, I pray to You to wash away from me all sin and transgression, all sadness and sorrow.

Master of the world, in whose hand are the souls of all living beings, grant me, my husband, (my family), all my relatives, and the totality of the Jewish people, Your blessings for long life, health, happiness, and good fortune (and satisfaction from their children). May Your pure spirit and Your Holy *Shechinah*, Divine Presence, rest upon me.

May it be Your will that our house be a house of peace, love, and brotherhood. May Your grace never depart from us, and may I always be worthy of the purity appropriate to the women of Your nation, the House of Israel. Amen.

---

1. Laminated checklist and prayer card is available from Jewish Marriage Education (see last page of book).

תפילה לפני הטבילה

רִבּוֹנוֹ שֶׁל עוֹלָם, בְּלֵב רָגִישׁ אֲנִי מְקַיֶּמֶת מִצְוַת טְבִילָה לְשֵׁם טָהֳרָה. הִשְׁתַּדַּלְתִּי לִהְיוֹת נֶאֱמָנָה לְמִצְוֹתֶיךָ וּמְצַפָּה לִישׁוּעָתֶךָ. וּכְשֵׁם שֶׁמֵּי הַמִּקְוֶה מְטַהֲרִים אוֹתִי מִבְּחִינָה רוּחָנִית, כָּךְ אֲנִי מִתְפַּלֶּלֶת אֵלֶיךָ שֶׁתִּשְׁטוֹף מֵעָלַי כָּל עֲבֵרָה וְעָווֹן וְכָל עֶצֶב וְיָגוֹן.

רִבּוֹנוֹ שֶׁל עוֹלָם, אֲשֶׁר בְּיָדְךָ נֶפֶשׁ כָּל חַי, חוֹנֵן אוֹתִי וְאֶת בַּעֲלִי (וּבְנֵי מִשְׁפַּחְתִּי) וְאֶת כָּל קְרוֹבַי וְאֶת כָּל עַם יִשְׂרָאֵל מִבִּרְכוֹתֶיךָ, לְחַיִּים אֲרֻכִּים בְּרִיאוּת אוֹשֶׁר וּמַזָּל טוֹב (וְנַחַת מִבָּנִים), וְתַשְׁרֶה עָלַי אֶת רוּחֲךָ הַטְּהוֹרָה וּשְׁכִינַת קָדְשֶׁךָ.

וִיהִי רָצוֹן שֶׁיְּהֵא בֵּיתֵנוּ בַּיִת שֶׁל שָׁלוֹם, אַהֲבָה וְאַחֲוָה, וְחַסְדְּךָ לֹא יָסוּר מֵעִמָּנוּ נֶצַח, וְאֶהְיֶה תָּמִיד רְאוּיָה לְטָהֳרָה הָרְאוּיָה לִנְשֵׁי עַמְּךָ בֵּית יִשְׂרָאֵל, אָמֵן.

Chapter 9

Taking the Plunge

The Proper Time for Tevilah — Immersion in the Mikveh

1. AT THE END OF the seven spotless nights and days, a woman is obligated to immerse in the *mikveh*. For example: If the *hefsek taharah* was performed on Monday afternoon, the next day, Tuesday, would be the first of the seven spotless days. The following Monday night would be the time for immersion. In other words, *ohr le*, the beginning of, Tuesday (for a further explanation of *ohr le*, see chapter 10).

2. A woman should only immerse in the *mikveh* at night after *tzeit hakochavim*, when at least three medium-size stars are visible. This law applies even when, for some valid reason, she is forced to postpone her immersion. If it is totally impossible to immerse at night, a Rav must be consulted.

3. If a woman's husband is out of town, it is preferable that she postpone her immersion until his return. Neverthe-

less, the halachah allows her to immerse also in his absence. If there is a chance that he may arrive suddenly or at a time she would be unable to immerse, she should not postpone her immersion.

4. It is a mitzvah to immerse on time. This also applies on Friday night if a woman's husband is in town. However, she should not immerse Friday night if her husband is not in town.

5. A woman who was scheduled to immerse before Friday night and postponed her immersion without a valid reason may not immerse Friday night. Nevertheless, it is advisable to consult a Rav in such a case.

6. On Yom Kippur night, Tishah B'Av night, and during her *shivah* week of mourning, a woman may not immerse, even if it is her appropriate time.

7. A husband planning an out-of-town trip should try to postpone his departure if he had intended to be away from home at the time of his wife's immersion.

The Laws of Chafifah — the Preparations Which Precede Immersion

The mitzvah of immersion requires a thorough preparation before immersing in the *mikveh*. This process of preparation is referred to as *chafifah*. It involves:

1. thorough bathing;

2. inspecting oneself for any possible *chatzitzot* — objects which prevent total body contact with the *mikveh* waters.

The halachah requires that at the time of immersion, the woman's entire body be submerged in the *mikveh*'s water. Nothing should separate her from the waters. Even though the body's "hidden parts" need not come into actual contact with the water, they too must be *chatzitzah*-free, i.e., with no intervening objects. This applies to a woman's mouth, teeth, nose, eyes, ears, nipples, navel, vagina, and anus. She must remove all intervening objects from these areas before immersion.

The Preparation Process

1. A woman must remove all hairpins and unbraid her hair. She must wash her hair with warm water and shampoo. Afterwards, she should carefully comb out her hair while wet, removing any knots. She should comb or separate by hand other body hair, including eyebrows, eyelashes, underarm and pubic hair.

2. It is proper for a woman to bathe in a bathtub for about half an hour, washing all parts of her body with warm water and soap (only soaps which rinse off totally should be used). The entire preparation process should take about an hour. In time of great urgency, half an hour is sufficient. If such a case should occur, extra care should be taken with the inspection of the body afterward. (When bathing in a bathtub is absolutely impossible, a woman may take a shower. However, this should be done meticulously, using sufficient soap and water.)

3. Ideally, a woman should begin the *chafifah* by day, carrying on till the time of immersion at night. If a woman cannot begin by day, she may bathe at night, preferably for an hour. Obviously it is better to bathe relaxedly and slowly at night than to bathe in a hurry during the day. Nevertheless, ideally, she should carry out at least one form of preparation during the day (for example, cutting her nails or washing her hair).

4. Bathing should be done as close to the time of immersing as possible.

5. It is customary to wash and comb at the *mikveh*. All *mikvaot* provide proper facilities for bathing. Nevertheless, a woman may prepare herself at home and then comb out her hair again at the *mikveh*.

6. Meat and chicken should not be eaten on the day of immersion because particles may stick between teeth and be difficult to remove. If the night of her immersion falls on *motza'ei Shabbat* or *yom tov* (on Shabbat and *yom tov* eating meat is a mitzvah), or if a woman forgot this restriction and ate meat, she must clean her teeth with extra care.

7. A woman should not knead dough with her hands on the day of her immersion. If it was *erev Shabbat* and she customarily bakes her own challah, or if she forgot and kneaded dough, she must take extra care to clean all particles of dough from her hands.

8. A woman should not eat between the *chafifah* and the *tevilah*, immersion.

9. Both fingernails and toenails must be cut and cleaned before immersion. One must be careful not to forget a nail or part of it. In certain instances, when a woman insists on keeping her nails long, a Rav must be consulted. Under the nails must be cleaned well in any case. One must remove nail polish, false nails, and the like.

10. A woman should blow her nose and use the bathroom, when necessary, before immersion.

11. All jewelry (earrings, rings, etc.), contact lenses, glasses, makeup, creams, and band-aids should be removed.

12. The ears, including earring holes, should be cleaned thoroughly.

13. The teeth must be brushed. In addition to a toothbrush, a toothpick or dental floss (only if she is used to using it) should be used. All removable false teeth should be taken out before immersion.

14. A woman is obligated to inspect (by looking at and feeling wherever she can't see) her body and hair before immersing to verify that there is no *chatzitzah*. This inspection is imperative; neglecting to inspect invalidates her immersion.

15. Immersion on Friday night requires special attention because of the laws of Shabbat. A woman may not bathe and comb her hair too late on Friday lest she violate the Shabbat. She may bathe at the *mikveh*, but she must be careful to finish a couple of minutes before sunset. Her husband can light the candles for her or she can light earlier than usual (but no earlier than 1¼ hours before sunset), "on condition" that she does not accept upon herself the onset of Shabbat until the correct time. Before sunset she should say, "I hereby accept upon myself the sanctity of Shabbat."

    Another option: that she bathes at home before the onset of Shabbat, lights candles at the correct time, then goes to the *mikveh* only to immerse.

16. Immersion on *motza'ei Shabbat*, Saturday night: preferably the *chafifah* should be done on Friday afternoon and then repeated *motza'ei Shabbat*. If that is impossible, it may all be done on *motza'ei Shabbat*. However, in such an instance, a woman should bathe for an hour before immersing.

17. A woman whose immersion is scheduled for a Friday night which follows a two-day *yom tov* should consult a Rav for instructions as to how and when to do the *chafifah*.

18. The process of *chafifah* should be done calmly and with ease. Do not rush! Relax!

Laws of Chatzitzah

A kosher immersion in the *mikveh* requires that every part of the body comes into contact with the water. All *chatzitzot* must be removed. Some examples of common types of *chatzitzot* are discussed below. Obviously, this book cannot cover all possible situations of *chatzizah* that may arise. One should always consult a Rav when in doubt.

Chatzitzot of the Hair

Body hair: A woman who regularly removes certain body hair before immersion — for example, shaving underarms, tweezing eyebrows, or waxing legs — must always do so before immersion. (For her own convenience it is worthwhile not to get used to regularly removing hair specifically at this time, so that it will not be considered a *chatzitzah*.) Women from *Eidot HaMizrach* customarily remove underarm and pubic hair before immersion. When one is particular to remove hair, it should preferably be done a day or two before immersion.

Dandruff or lice: A woman must do the maximum to remove excess dandruff or lice before immersion.

Dyes: Some hair dyes are considered *chatzitzot*. The decision depends on the substance used as a dye, therefore a Rav must be consulted.

Hair conditioner: It is preferable not to use hair conditioner prior to immersion.

Chatzitzot of the Body

Callouses and hardened skin: The determination of whether or not these are considered a *chatzitzah* depends on the woman's attitude. If she normally removes them, she must remove them as she usually does. If she does not usually bother to remove them, they are not considered a *chatzitzah* for her.

Color stains on the skin (e.g., ink, blood, milk, paint): If the woman would not normally mind the stain, it is only considered a *chatzitzah* if dry or if the blood is sticky. In such an instance, she must soften it in warm water. If she would normally be disturbed by such a stain and attempt to remove it, it is considered a *chatzitzah* whether dry or moist. She must then scrub it off as best she can. Any residue is not considered a *chatzitzah*.

Discharge from a sore: A dry or sticky discharge is considered a *chatzitzah*; a moist discharge is not.

Ears and nose: A dry discharge found on the outer ear or outer nose is considered a *chatzitzah*; on the inner area, it is not. All discharge should be removed from the openings of the ears or nose.

Eyes: Any discharge found on the outside of the eye, whether dry or moist, is considered a *chatzitzah*. Inside the eye, a dry discharge is considered a *chatzitzah*, a moist one is not.

Hanging skin: Remove whatever possible and the rest is not a *chatzitzah*. Specifically remove big pieces of skin. Peeling skin should be smoothed, and only skin which bothers the woman should be removed. The remainder which does not bother her may be left as is.

Pus: Pus which is in a sore beneath the skin is not considered a *chatzitzah*. Different rules apply if it is on the surface of the skin. For the first three days of the wound, the pus is not considered a *chatzitzah* if moist. Afterwards, or when dry, it is considered a *chatzitzah* and must be softened well by soaking in water.

Scabs: A scab covering a wound that has not yet healed should be softened well by soaking in water. It is not considered a *chatzitzah* and need not be removed. If the sore has healed, the scab is a *chatzitzah* and must be removed.

Splinters: A splinter beneath the skin is not considered a *chatzitzah*. On the skin surface or above, it is considered a *chatzitzah*.

Teeth: Permanent fillings, caps, or bridges are not considered *chatzitzot*. But if possible she should clean well under the bridge. A Rav should be consulted in regard to temporary fillings or caps.

In general, the definition of what constitutes a *chatzitzah* is as follows: Anything that most women are particular to remove, even if only occasionally, and even if an individual woman is not bothered by it, is considered a *chatzitzah*. In addition anything than an individual woman is particular to remove even though most woman are not bothered by it, for this individual woman this is considered a *chatzitzah*.

Laws of Tevilah

1. Upon completing her bathing preparations and inspecting herself for any *chatzitzot*, she must immerse her entire body in a kosher *mikveh*. The *mikveh* must contain enough water to reach at least 24–30 cm. (9.5–12 inches) above her navel when she is standing erect. A very short woman should stand on a wide step if possible.

2. In order to ensure that her body and hair are totally sub-

merged in the *mikveh*, an attendant (a Jewish female above the age of twelve) supervises the immersion. If no attendant is available, the woman should consult a Rav.

3. At the time of immersion the *mikveh* waters must reach all parts of her body, therefore the body should be relaxed.

    In addition, a woman should not:
    a) hold on to anyone or press forcefully against the wall;
    b) clench her fists or feet;
    c) close her lips very tightly;
    d) shut her eyes very tightly.

    In case of problematic situations (e.g., a woman physically unable to support herself or afraid of submerging in water), a Rav should be consulted for a possible solution. (It is worthwhile to note that a *mikveh* specially designed to be used by women who are physically disabled and unable to walk was constructed in Jerusalem.)

4. A woman should not immerse totally upright nor very bent. Rather, she should lean forward slightly as if kneading dough. Her legs and arms should be in a normal walking position and not close against her body.

5. After immersing once, a woman recites the following blessing:

בָּרוּךְ אַתָּה ה' אֱלֹקֵינוּ מֶלֶךְ הָעוֹלָם אֲשֶׁר קִדְּשָׁנוּ בְּמִצְוֹתָיו וְצִוָּנוּ עַל הַטְּבִילָה.

Blessed are You, G-d, our Lord, King of the world, who has sanctified us with His commandments and commanded us concerning immersion.

After reciting the blessing, she should immerse again. It is proper that she has the intention that her immersion is for the sake of purification. It is common practice to immerse three times. (Some woman follow different customs which require additional immersions.)

While reciting the blessing —

a) she should not look into the water, so that she does not see her nakedness;

b) she should fold her arms under her heart so as to separate the upper and lower parts of the body; she should try to see that the palms of her hands do not touch her body;

c) some follow the custom to cover their head with a towel.

The custom of some women from *Eidot HaMizrach* is to recite the blessing before entering the room of the *mikveh*, while they are still covered with a towel.

6. The *mikveh* attendant confirms the immersion by pronouncing "kosher," meaning the immersion was performed properly.

The act of immersion should be kept as a private matter between husband and wife. One should try, wherever feasible, to keep it from others.

Upon greeting her husband after immersing, a woman should inform him that she has immersed (verbally or by some other indication). Just as she previously announced to him her entry into the state of *niddah*, so now she informs him of her change of status to that of *taharah*.

At times when a regular *mikveh* is unavailable, a Rav should be consulted for instructions concerning the use of other acceptable bodies of water (e.g., spring-fed lakes or the sea). These alternatives should only be used under exceptional circumstances. In these instances:

1. Do not stand in a narrow place or step where the possibility of falling exists.
2. Follow the Rav's instructions concerning a suitable place to stand when immersing.
3. Choose a quiet and private area for the immersion.

The Mikveh Attendant

Although it is every woman's personal responsibility to wash and inspect herself in preparation for immersion, the halachah requires that at the time of immersion a Jewish woman be available to supervise the immersion, assuring that it has been performed properly, and that the whole body has immersed at one time, so that not even a single hair floats above the water. This woman, called the *mikveh* attendant, is also available to assist the woman in her preparations prior to immersion.

Suggested List of Items to Bring to the Mikveh[1]

- back brush
- *bedikah* cloths
- clean pair of colored underpants
- comb
- dental floss or toothpicks
- hair brush
- handkerchief or tissues
- makeup remover
- money (for *mikveh* fee and telephones)
- nail brush
- nail filer
- nail polish remover
- pumice stone
- Q-tips
- rubber slippers
- scissors
- scrubbing sponge
- shampoo
- small mirror
- soap
- toothbrush
- toothpaste
- towel

1. Many *mikvaot* supply some of these items, so verify the necessity to bring your own.

Checklist of Preparations before Immersion[2]

- remove any hair that is generally removed (preferably not on the day of immersion)
- cut and file nails
- remove nail polish
- remove makeup
- clean ears and earring holes
- clean eyes, eyebrows, lashes
- blow and clean nose
- wash hair
- clean teeth; use toothpick/floss
- clean breast nipples
- clean navel
- wash entire body — pay attention to elbows, knees, spaces between fingers and toes, and the back
- smooth hard skin
- wash genital areas, also internally
- comb all hair
- check entire body
- use bathroom if needed
- remove all jewelry, glasses, lenses, false teeth

---

2. A laminated checklist for immersion can be obtained from Jewish Marriage Education (see last page of book).

Chapter 10

A Little Mathematics

Hilchot Onot: The Laws of Onot

HILCHOT ONOT deal with certain precautions that must be taken on the days when the woman anticipates the onset of menstruation. The purpose of these laws is to prevent marital relations from taking place on days when the woman could get her period. These laws are called *hilchot onot* because they deal with the day or night that the woman is likely to begin menstruating. These laws prevent the couple from violating the severe prohibition of *niddah*.

Most women nowadays do not menstruate regularly at an exact predetermined day and hour. Nevertheless, there are certain patterns which one can observe. The following laws provide a woman with guidelines in recognizing those patterns and defining and calculating her *onot*.

The laws of *Taharat HaMishpachah* obligate every Jewish woman to calculate her *onot*. Everyone can calculate them on her own, even those who shy away from numbers and calculations. Another possibility for a woman who is apprehensive is to calculate her *onot* together with her husband. After all, two heads are better than one. In cases of difficulty, do not hesitate to consult a Rav. Be assured, however, that for many generations, women who did not possess an academic degree in mathematics and who never even graduated high school have been able to calculate their *onot*.

The following definitions are important in order to understand these laws:

Onah: the day or night that a woman can be expected to begin her *veset*, menstrual period.

Day: the time from sunrise to sunset.

Night: the time from sunset to sunrise.

The above definitions apply in both the summer (when the days are longer) and the winter (when days are shorter).

To observe the laws of *onot*, every woman must keep a personal account of the Hebrew calendar date, and the *onah* (whether by day or by night) on which her period began. (Also any specific signs accompanying the onset of her period.) The use of a Hebrew calendar is essential for these calculations. There is no way these laws can be kept without it.

An example of the Hebrew calendar date (which is calculated from sunset to sunset):

TammuzJuly

11 Wednesday 8

12 Thursday 9

Sunset this Wednesday is 6:50 p.m. If a woman began to menstruate on Wednesday, July 8th, at 4:00 p.m., the Hebrew date would be the 11th of Tammuz. But if she got her period on Wednesday, July 8th, at 7:00 p.m., the Hebrew date would be the 12th of Tammuz, accurately called the beginning of, *ohr le*, 12th of Tammuz.

It must be emphasized that the *onah* is determined by the time, whether day or night, in addition to the date on which a woman began to menstruate, i.e., if menstruation began by day, her *onah* is by day, and if menstruation began by night, her *onah* is by night.

The time menstruation began is determined according to the *onah* when the woman saw the blood. For example, if she wakes up in the morning after sunrise and sees blood, even though it could well be that her period began at night, we calculate according to the time she actually saw the menstrual blood, in this case by day.

The Precautions at the Time of the Onah

The following precautions must be taken at the time of the *onah*:

1. *Perishah*, separation — marital relations during the *onah* are forbidden. It is preferable to be stringent and not to hug, kiss, and obviously not to sleep in the same bed. All other forms of interaction are permissible.

2. A *bedikah*, an internal inspection — the same as performed during the seven spotless days, a *bedikah* is obligatory on the *onah*. It is better to do it towards the end of the *onah*. Preferably one should do two *bedikot*. If a woman's *onah* is by day, she does one *bedikah* in the morning and one before sunset. If a woman's *onah* is by night, she should do one *bedikah* at night and one upon rising in the morning. If a woman's *onah* passes without the onset of menstruation, and she did not do a *bedikah* on her *onah*, she should do one as soon as she remembers.

3. It is better to shower rather than bathe in a tub during the *onah*, but if bathing in a tub is desired, the required *bedikah* should be carried out beforehand.

Calculating Onot

The calculation of *onot* is based on the nature of a woman's menstrual cycle. There are two categories of periods: the *veset kavua*, regular period, and the *veset lo kavua*, irregular period.

The Veset Kavua — Regular Period

This is established when menstruation occurs for three successive months at a fixed time as defined by the halachah. In fact there are thirteen types of regular periods but we will mention only the more well-known ones:

- *veset hachodesh kavua* — a regular "Hebrew date" period is determined when the period began three successive times on the same *onah* and on the same Hebrew date.
- *veset haflagah kavua* — a regular "interval" period is determined when the period began three successive times on the same *onah* and after three identical intervals, i.e., three consecutive times the number of days between the beginning of one period and the beginning of the next one is the same.
- *veset haguf kavua* — a regular "bodily symptom" period is determined by specific bodily symptoms which regularly appear before the period begins.
- *veset al yedei maaseh* — a regular "particular activity" period is determined by a particular activity being the cause for the period to begin.

The latter two examples are determined by the occurrence of the period three consecutive times but it makes no difference in what *onah*.

Sometimes a woman's period is established according to both a fixed time and a fixed physical symptom.

All the regular periods are nullified when, for three successive months, menstruation does not begin on the expected date. A Rav must be consulted to verify the establishment (or cancellation) of the regular period, for the laws are extremely detailed.

It must be emphasized that nowadays, the regular period is quite a rare phenomenon.

On her *onah*, a woman with a regular period must follow the precautions involving *perishah*, separation, and *bedikot*, internal inspections, described above.

The Veset Lo Kavua — Irregular Period

The menstrual cycles of most women today fit into this category. (This is true even if they get their period at approximately the same time monthly.) When is the *onah* of such women? The following section describes the calculations that such women must make to determine their *onot*.

Note: Often one *onah* falls on the same date as another *onah*.

Important to remember: All calculations are from the first day of the last period and, obviously, are according to the Hebrew calendar date, which is from sunset to sunset.

Onot on Which the Precautions Are Required for a Woman with an Irregular Period

1. *Onat Haflagah* — the Interval *Onah*: the number of days between her last two menstrual periods. In calculating this interval a woman counts from the first day of her second to last period to the first day of her last period. Included in this count are the first days of both periods. (To demonstrate: the interval between the thumb and the pinky as calculated this way would be five.) This *onah*

will either be by day or by night, depending on when her last period began.

Example: A woman's second to last period began on the 1st of Tammuz as a night *onah* (i.e., *ohr le* 1st Tammuz). Her last period began on the 3rd of Av by day. The interval between them is thirty-two days. Therefore her interval *onah* will be on the 4th of Elul by day, thirty-two days after the 3rd of Av.

2. *Onat Hachodesh* — the Monthly *Onah*: the Hebrew calendar date on which menstruation began the previous month. This *onah* will be either by day or by night, depending on when her last period began.

   Example: A woman's previous menstrual period began on the 13th of Tishrei by day. Therefore her monthly *onah* will be on the 13th of Cheshvan by day.

   (Some are stringent and observe also the *onah* before the *onat haflagah* and the *onah* before the *onat hachodesh*. That is, they keep the laws of *onot* also on the day or night before the *onah*. If this happens to come out on a woman's immersion night or wedding night, or her husband is about to travel out of town, she does not follow this stringency; instead, she does a *bedikah* and is then permitted to him.)

3. *Onah Beinonit* — the Common *Onah*: the 30th day from the first day of a woman's last menstrual period. According to many authorities, it is preferable to regard the 31st day also as the *onah beinonit* and observe the laws of *onot* then as well. This *onah* lasts twenty-four hours for the 30th day: a night and day on the Hebrew calendar (and twenty-four hours for the 31st day, i.e., forty-eight hours when observing both days).

   Example: A woman's last period began on the 23rd

of Shevat. The 30th day is the night and day of the 22nd of Adar (and the 31st day is the night and day of the 23rd of Adar).[1]

(Some authorities hold that a woman who never menstruates until after the 30th day is not obligated to keep the *onah beinonit*.)

An additional rule applies to a woman whose period always begins after an interval differing by no more than three days; for example, if she always begins menstruating after 26 or 27 or 28 days from her last period. This woman, in addition to keeping the above *onot*, must do a *bedikah* before marital relations on any of these three days that are not the days of her *onah*.[2]

4. *Onat Haguf* — menstruation that begins immediately after the appearance of specific bodily symptoms. A woman who experiences specific physical symptoms immediately prior to the onset of her period must observe as an *onah* the day or night when these symptoms occur. (This does not refer to the various aches and pains which commonly precede the onset of a woman's period — such as headaches and the like — and which occur at other times too.) This type of *onah* is quite rare, and requires consultation with a Rav in order to determine it.

---

1. Hebrew months have either twenty-nine or thirty days. Whenever a Hebrew month has twenty-nine days, the 30th day (observed as the *onah beinonit* by all) and the *onat hachodesh* will be the same. Whenever a Hebrew month has thirty days, the 31st day (when observed as the *onah beinonit*) and the *onat hachodesh* will be on the same day.

2. There are some who are very stringent and separate for as many days as she had heavy bleeding during the previous period.

Laws of Onot Applying to Women Who Are Mesulakot Damim — Those Who Do Not Usually Menstruate

Our Sages have determined three situations which place women in this category:

1. *Pregnancy:* A woman who does not see blood during pregnancy is not required to observe *onot*. (The halachic definition of pregnancy is after three months.) A woman who does see blood during pregnancy becomes a *niddah* and she must make a *hefsek taharah*, count seven spotless days, and immerse. She must observe the *onot* according to the laws of a woman with an irregular period. This applies even if she had a regular period and she sees blood on days which would have been her regular period.

   The following laws apply to a pregnant woman who does not see blood in pregnancy: A woman with an irregular period must observe her *onot* in the first month of pregnancy only. A woman with a regular period must observe her *onah* on the appropriate day for the first three months (in order to cancel her *chazakah*). Excluded is a woman with a regular interval period, who does not need to take precautions after the first month.

2. *Childbirth:* A woman who gives birth (or miscarries) need not observe the laws of *onah* during the first twenty-four months after giving birth unless she sees blood. Should she see blood within these twenty-four months, she must observe the *onah* laws of a woman with an irregular period.

   (If a woman had a regular period before giving birth, according to the halachah, she returns to her regular period only after twenty-four months. Nowadays, however, it is customary for her to return to her regular period also during these twenty-four months.)

3. *Menopause*:

Around the age of 50 — Nowadays menstruation does not cease all at once but rather it ceases and then reappears after a while, then ceases again for a longer time, until it ceases completely. Therefore, a woman who did not have a regular period before menopause need not keep any *onot* once she stops menstruating. Should she menstruate again, she must observe the laws of *onot* as for an irregular period. It is preferable that for half a year after menses have ceased she should check herself before marital relations.

A woman who had a regular period before menopause continues to observe her usual *onah* until the menses do not occur for six months. If she menstruates after this point, she continues to keep *onah* laws as for an irregular period.

Around the age of 60 — A woman who has ceased menstruating totally, and three months have passed since she last menstruated, does not keep any *onah* at all. This is so whether beforehand she had a regular or irregular period. If she sees blood again she should contact a Rav.

A Sample Calendar for Practice

A. A woman got her period Saturday, the 1st of Nissan, March 19, at 4:00 p.m. (Sunset is at 6:00 p.m.) Thus, her *onah* is by day.

Onot for Iyar are as follows:

B. *Onah Beinonit* — Common *Onah*. 30th day = 30th of Nissan, Sunday, April 17. *Onah* extends from sunset Saturday until sunset Sunday.

C. 31st day = 1st of Iyar, Monday, April 18. *Onah* extends from sunset Sunday until sunset Monday.

D. *Onat Hachodesh* — Monthly *Onah*. 1st of Iyar, Monday, April 18. *Onah* extends from sunrise until sunset.

Month of Iyar

E. The woman's next period began on Monday night, April 18, at 7:00 p.m. which is the beginning of Tuesday, the 2nd of Iyar. (Sunset is at 6:20 p.m.) Thus, her *onah* is at night.

Onot for Sivan are as follows:

F. *Onah Beinonit* — Common *Onah*. 30th day = 2nd of Sivan, Wednesday, May 18. *Onah* extends from sunset Tuesday until sunset Wednesday.

G. 31st day = 3rd of Sivan, Thursday, May 19. *Onah* extends from sunset Wednesday until sunset Thursday.

H. *Onat Hachodesh* — Monthly *Onah*. 2nd of Sivan, Wednesday, May 18. *Onah* extends from sunset Tuesday, until sunrise Wednesday.

Hebrew calendar dates are in bold; English calendar dates are regular.

Month of March — Adar/Nissan						
Sun	Mon	Tue	Wed	Thu	Fri	Sat
			1	2	3	4	5
	6	7	8	9	10	11	12
	13	14	15	16	17	18	**1** ^A 19
2 20	**3** 21	**4** 22	**5** 23	**6** 24	**7** 25	**8** 26
9 27	**10** 28	**11** 29	**12** 30	**13** 31		

Month of April — Nissan/Iyar						
Sun	Mon	Tue	Wed	Thu	Fri	Sat
					14 1	**15** 2
16 3	**17** 4	**18** 5	**19** 6	**20** 7	**21** 8	**22** 9
23 10	**24** 11	**25** 12	**26** 13	**27** 14	**28** 15	**29** 16
30 17	^B**1** 18	^C**2** ^D**E** 19	**3** 20	**4** 21	**5** 22	**6** 23
7 24	**8** 25	**9** 26	**10** 27	**11** 28	**12** 29	**13** 30

Month of May — Iyar/Sivan						
Sun	Mon	Tue	Wed	Thu	Fri	Sat
14 1	**15** 2	**16** 3	**17** 4	**18** 5	**19** 6	**20** 7
21 8	**22** 9	**23** 10	**24** 11	**25** 12	**26** 13	**27** 14
28 15	**29** 16	**1** 17	**2** ^F 18	**3** ^H**G** 19	**4** ^I 20	**5** 21
6 22	**7** 23	**8** 24	**9** 25	**10** 26	**11** 27	**12** 28
13 29	**14** 30	**15** 31				

I. *Onat Haflagah* — Interval *Onah*. Interval between periods is thirty two days. 4th of Sivan, Friday, May 20th. *Onah* extends from sunset Thursday until sunrise Friday.

Sample Page from a Personal Calendar[3]

SEP/OCT '02 — TISHREI 5763 — תשרי תשס״ג

INSTRUCTIONS:

1. Please carefully study the filled out sample entry page with its corresponding entries on the sample Tishrei (Sept/Oct) calendar.

2. Following the instructions on the entry page, take care to enter the pertinent information during the course of the month.

3. Indicate on the corresponding calendar in accordance with the sample format.

4. Once this has been done, consult your calendar page and this will give you easy, clear-cut guidance to successful observance of the Mitzvah.

PLEASE NOTE:

☐ = Sunrise to sunset = (Day) ☐ = Sunset to sunrise = (Night)

Ohr le = The beginning of the Hebrew date (i.e. the night).

---

3. A personal calendar may be obtained from Jewish Marriage Education (see last page of book).

Chapter 11

Brides and Grooms

EVERY MARRIAGE IS considered a microcosm of the ultimate wedding relationship, the bond between G-d and the Jewish people, and every Jewish home is considered a miniature sanctuary. Thus, the couple's marriage day represents the day on which the *Shechinah*, the Divine Presence, descends to rest between them.

Accordingly, the day of a couple's wedding should be marked by appropriate behavior. In contrast to the reckless frivolity which sometimes characterizes many secular marriages, Jewish tradition views the wedding day as one of holiness and sanctity. Indeed, our Sages describe it as a personal Yom Kippur for the bride and groom. All their sins are forgiven, and they are given exceptional spiritual energies with which to face the new challenges married life will bring.

The wedding day should be set aside for *teshuvah* — repentance, *tefillah* — prayer, and *tzedakah* — charity. It is customary for both the bride and groom to fast on their wedding day. (If either fear that fasting will be too difficult, a Rav should be consulted.) The couple pray the afternoon prayers of *erev Yom Kippur* which include the *viduy*, the confessional prayers, and it is customary to ask one's parents for forgiveness. Moreover, the bride and groom should give generously to charity on their wedding day. Our Sages relate that in the midst of the busy preparations of her wedding day, Rabbi Akiva's daughter took time out to give a meal to a hungry wayfarer. The next morning a poisonous snake was found by her bed, pierced by her hair clip. Without knowing it, she had killed the snake when she took down her hair. Our Sages tell us that it was in the merit of her generosity on her wedding day that she was miraculously saved.

Laws Regarding a Bride and Groom

1. Every bride should consult a Rav or her *Taharat HaMishpachah* counselor to assist her in determining the date for her wedding.

2. As close as possible to the wedding date, every bride must make a *hefsek taharah* and count seven spotless days. She then immerses in a *mikveh*.

3. Preferably, the immersion should be on the night before the wedding. In any case, one should try to see that the immersion should not take place more than four days before the wedding.

4. A bride may immerse on the eighth day, during the day, after the seven spotless days. If the wedding coincides with the seventh day of the seven spotless days, a Rav should be consulted as to the time of immersion.

5. The bride must preferably continue to do one *bedikah* every day until, and including, the wedding day.[1]

---

1. The Ashkenazic custom is that the bride and groom refrain from seeing each other prior to the wedding from the time she does the *hefsek taharah*. The Sephardic custom places no restriction on the bride and groom seeing each other, even on the day of the wedding.

6. After marital relations have taken place, a virgin bride is considered a *niddah* whether she discovers hymenal bleeding or not. (If there is a doubt whether complete marital relations have taken place, one must consult a Rav, who will take into consideration factors such as painful sensations and the presence of blood.)

7. After marital relations have taken place, a virgin bride need only wait *four* days before making a *hefsek taharah* and counting seven spotless days prior to immersing in a *mikveh*. If she menstruates in the meantime, she must wait at least *five* days from the day she saw hymenal bleeding before performing the *hefsek taharah* and counting seven spotless days.

8. Upon marriage, a woman must create a *chazakah*, verification, that marital relations do not induce menstruation. She does this by performing a *bedikah*, prior to and following marital relations, at the first three opportunities she has after hymenal bleeding has ceased, preferably on her "unsafe" days.

   What are her "unsafe days"? Most women who do not have a regular period nevertheless have a fixed number of days before which they never expect their period. For example: a woman does not get her period before the 25th day from her last period, but after the 25th day she could get her period at any time. The days from her immersion until the 25th day are considered her "safe days," while the days after the 25th day are called her "unsafe" days.

   Bedieved, after the event, if she did a *bedikah* on her safe days, it can be relied on to create her *chazakah*.

   (During her "safe days" she is compared to a woman with a regular period who is not obligated to do a *bedikah* before and after marital relations. But when her "unsafe days" begin, she is compared to a woman with an irregular period, and she must do a *bedikah* the first three times before and after marital relations. Her husband must also check himself at these three times.)

After creating this *chazakah* (completing this process of verification that marital relations not cause them to see blood) the couple need not check themselves further. They may rest assured that marital relations do not cause the woman to menstruate.

A woman who sees blood after marital relations (after her hymenal bleeding has totally ceased) should consult a doctor and a Rav. If this occurs once after marital relations, she should check herself the next time after marital relations.

Chupat Niddah — A Wedding Conducted While the Bride Is a Niddah

When a bride is a *niddah* on the wedding night, the couple may not engage in any intimacy. All laws of *yichud* apply to them until the bride has immersed. There are various halachic options available under these circumstances, when they are forbidden to spend the night alone, and a Rav should be consulted to determine the best halachic solution for each couple.

The occurrence of a *chupat niddah* is obviously something every bride and groom tries to avoid. Therefore the bride should keep a personal calendar before marriage and should get advice in planning the date of her wedding.

The practice of taking hormone pills to avoid a *chupat niddah* may sometimes be permitted, but it is definitely not encouraged. If the bride is considering taking the pill before the wedding (in a case of a definite *chupat niddah* or when in doubt), she should discuss the matter seriously with a Rav and a doctor. (It must be noted that some hormone pills cause the opposite result, as they are likely to cause staining.)

When it happens that the bride is a *niddah* at the wedding, the couple should remember that this is the will of Providence. Thousands of couples have faced this challenge, and, as our Sages teach, "G-d does not come to His creations with overburdening demands" (*Avodah Zarah* 3a). Whenever G-d presents man with a trial, He provides him with the inner strength to overcome it. The couple should remember that this challenge too lasts only a few days and their whole life is still before them.

Chapter 12

Childbirth and Childbearing

Laws Concerning Childbirth

1. A WOMAN IN labor, prior to actual childbirth, is considered a *niddah* from the moment her contractions are so intense or so frequent that she feels the need to lie down or she cannot walk around anymore.

2. The show of blood which often precipitates the onset of labor renders a woman a *niddah*.

3. The breaking of the bag of waters does not necessarily render a woman a *niddah*. For determination, a Rav should be consulted.

4. Childbirth itself renders a woman a *niddah*.

5. Once a woman enters the *niddah* state for any of the above reasons, all the *harchakot* that are generally observed must be followed. Thus, her husband may not look at the parts of her body that are usually covered, and he may not touch her or hand objects directly to her.

6. According to the halachah, a woman may immerse in the *mikveh* on completion of seven days after the birth of

a son and on completion of fourteen days after the birth of a daughter, provided she has made a *hefsek taharah* and counted seven spotless days.

Practically, most women find that they cannot successfully perform a *hefsek taharah* until at least six to eight weeks after childbirth. (This coincides with most medical advice, which suggests that a woman wait until her postnatal checkup — six weeks after childbirth — to resume marital relations.) If three months have passed, and a woman is still unable to count seven spotless days, she should consult a doctor and a Rav.

7. In case of a miscarriage, a woman may immerse in the *mikveh* on completion of seven days if the fetus could be determined to be male. If it was female or the gender could not be determined, the completion of fourteen days is required before immersion. Needless to say, the above only applies provided the woman has performed a *hefsek taharah* and has counted seven spotless days.

Concerning Birth Control

RABBI COHEN WAS INVITED to lecture at a women's convention. At one of the sessions, the topic concerned the pursuit of a career outside the home. The Rabbi kept the audience spellbound, elaborating on the fulfilment, joy, growth, and satisfaction a woman can find within her own home. He did not rule out the possibility of an outside career, but only provided the woman has her priorities in the right order and recognizes her responsibilities at home.

One woman in the audience found Rabbi Cohen's ideas difficult to accept. She had been trained to look at motherhood as a burdensome yoke to be handled without affecting the woman's

professional career, which marched forward toward "liberation."
"Rabbi," she said, requesting the floor, "pardon me for being so
nosy, but what does your wife do?"

"My wife?" the Rabbi exclaimed. "Why, she runs a children's
shelter for eight children. She tends to their physical, emotional,
and psychological needs. She monitors their growth, enriches
their learning experiences, and encourages their creativity
within the capabilities of each child. She also plays the role of
teacher, nurse, companion, and cook, among others, and it's all
done with devotion and joy!"

The audience applauded as a sign of appreciation. Here was a
truly liberated woman, dedicating her abilities and skills to bene-
fit unfortunate children.

"By the way," concluded Rabbi Cohen with a smile, "those
eight children are our own..."

The women could not help but grin sheepishly. They recog-
nized the absurdity of social standards that would consider the
Rabbi's wife's occupation as a respectable career provided it was
someone else's children she was raising, but not her own!

In contrast, the Torah regards motherhood and the role of
the homemaker with the utmost respect. The Torah encourages the woman to enjoy the blessing of children and not to
view the process of raising them as a heavy burden which dis-
turbs her own personal growth. Moreover, there is no greater
means of character development than being a wife and
mother. Through motherhood a woman develops all her inner strengths and brings the Divine Presence into her home.

The very first mitzvah in the Torah is "Be fruitful and multi-
ply and replenish the earth and subdue it" (*Bereishit* 1:28). G-d
grants every woman precisely the number of children she is
capable of raising. If she dedicates her life to the role of moth-

erhood, this will be positively reflected in her children, grand-children, and in their offspring for generations to come.

The Torah considers the presence of children as the very source of blessing in the home.

> *A man should wish for and desire offspring, beseeching G-d*
> *to bless him with a household of sons and daughters, for him*
> *to raise and guide to serve G-d.*
>
> *(Sefer HaKedushah)*

The Torah describes a natural, Divine plan for child spacing that works in accordance with a woman's physical makeup. Thus, a breast-feeding woman is referred to by the halachah as *mesuleket damim*, infertile, which in the past she usually was for as long as two years after childbirth. Even to-day, despite changes in nature, many women who breast-feed their children exclusively find that they often do not conceive during this time. However, even a woman who conceives while nursing should look upon the opportunity to bring an-other baby into the world as a Divine blessing.

Laws Concerning Birth Control

1. Birth control is not permitted unless a Rav is consulted and he specifically rules that a couple may use contra-ception. A husband and wife cannot rely upon a decision given to another couple.

2. One may not postpone the proper time for *mikveh* im-mersion for this purpose unless permitted to do so by a Rav.

3. The Torah's commandment, "...he shall live by them" (*Vayikra* 18:5), negates a life of suffering and misery. Therefore, a woman who has a physiological, psycho-logical, or emotional need to practice birth control,

should, together with her husband, consult a Rav. Only he is given halachic authority to decide when birth control may be practiced, for how long, and by which means.

To enable the Rav to come to the proper conclusion, he must be given all medical information. In addition, the woman should be sure to state to the Rav her specific problem, her feelings, and her needs. Thus, he will be in a position to render a decision in accordance with her personal situation. Each case must be viewed individually within the confines of the halachah because what may be a suitable solution for one couple may not be suitable for another.

One should constantly bear in mind that the all-encompassing task of raising children is acknowledged by thousands of families as the height of joy and fulfillment with no comparison to any other type of satisfaction. Raising children can certainly be considered a "profession," and a mother busy with this is surely worthy of the title "professional."

The difficulties and challenges entailed in this noteworthy profession should be viewed in light of the words of our Sages: "The reward comes in relation to the difficulties" (*Avot* 5:23). The reward for keeping a mitzvah is given according to the amount of difficulty there was in its observance. In addition to the *nachas* and pleasure derived from raising children in this world, a position of honor is reserved for the woman in the World to Come!

Index to Halachot

Appendix

Additions and Different Customs for Women from Eidot HaMizrach According to the Rulings of HaRav HaGaon Ovadia Yosef, shlita

CHAPTER 3: GETTING TO KNOW THE DIVINE IMAGE WITHIN YOU

p. 57. How does one determine the state of *niddah*? The law concerning the feeling of the passage of liquid is the same as the law of a stain. Details of these laws are explained on p. 58.

p. 59. Concerning discharges: The law concerning this feeling is the same as the law of a stain, as above.

p. 60. The size of a stain: The size of a *gris* is about 20 mm.

CHAPTER 5: THE COUNTDOWN

p. 80. When can a woman perform a *hefsek taharah*? The custom of Sephardim is on the fourth day from when she began to see blood.

p. 83. What is the right time of day for the *hefsek taharah bedikah*? She is obligated *lechatchilah* (preferably) before sunset. *Bedieved*, after the event, if she did the *bedikah* three or four minutes after sunset her *bedikah* is valid.

p. 84. What can be used for a *bedikah* cloth? Cotton wool can be used *lechatchilah*.

CHAPTER 7: KEEPING A DISTANCE

p. 104. Touching:

According to the custom of Sephardim, one can be lenient with passing a child when he is big enough and on his own goes over from the mother's lap to the father's lap or vice versa.

Sephardim are customarily lenient concerning the throwing of an object from the husband's hand to the wife's.

Sephardim are customarily lenient with the details of the laws of sitting on one seat that swings.

When traveling in a car on vacation, Sephardim are customarily lenient regarding sitting on one seat; it is preferable to put an object between them to prevent touching.

p. 106. Concerning pouring a drink or food for one another — Sephardim are customarily lenient in this.

p. 106. Concerning pouring wine: Sephardim are customarily lenient. However, when pouring wine with water one must be stringent and must make a change from the usual, both when the wife pours for her husband and when the husband pours for his wife.

p. 106. Concerning the separation of beds and bedding: It is good to be careful that their bedding does not touch.

p. 106. Concerning the woman lying on her husband's bed in

his presence: It is correct to be stringent with this.

p. 107. Concerning preparing water for washing and preparing a bath: Sephardim are customarily lenient with this. However, Sephardim are stringent when it comes to pouring the water on the other's body.

p. 107. Concerning smelling the perfume of the woman: It is praiseworthy that the husband be stringent and not intentionally smell his wife's perfume on her body or on her clothes.

p. 107. Concerning hearing his wife singing when she's a *niddah*: According to the law one may be lenient with this.

p. 107. Concerning the behavior of the couple when the wife is sick: One should not be lenient in order to feed her and lift her unless in a situation where there is a chance of danger. Passing an object from his hand to her hand or touching by means of another object is permitted even when there is no chance of danger.

In every instance it is desirable to ask a Rav how to behave.

CHAPTER 9: TAKING THE PLUNGE

p. 126. Concerning if it is permitted for her to immerse in his absence: It is praiseworthy to be stringent with this because there are those who say there is a danger involved.

p. 127. Concerning if she is permitted to immerse on Friday night if immersion has been postponed, Sephardim are customarily lenient with this.

p. 134. Concerning the blessing said on immersion: The blessing must be said in a room adjacent to the room of the *mikveh*, before immersion, when she is still wrapped in a towel or gown. Immediately following her reciting the blessing, she removes her gown, goes into the *mikveh*, and immerses once. She need not immerse more than that.

P. 135 The *mikveh* attendant confirms the immersion and holds out her hand to help her get out of the *mikveh*.

CHAPTER 10: A LITTLE MATHEMATICS

p. 141. Concerning bathing in the tub on the day she is anticipating her period: Some are stringent *lechatchilah* (preferably) not to bathe in a tub or swimming pool on the day of her *onah*. For medical purposes it is permitted.

p. 144. Concerning the time of the Common *Onah*, Sephardim are customarily lenient also with the common *onah* to keep one *onah* only, i.e., the day or the night, and they are not stringent to keep twenty-four hours. They are also not stringent to keep the 31st day as well.

CHAPTER 11: BRIDES AND GROOMS

p. 152. Concerning a bride who sees menstrual blood after seeing hymenal bleeding, according to the Sephardic custom she must wait four days from seeing hymenal bleeding.

CHAPTER 12: CHILDBIRTH AND CHILDBEARING

p. 155. Concerning the woman in labor, from when does she become forbidden to her husband? One can be lenient not to consider her a *niddah* as long as there is no discharge of blood and the birth has not actively begun.

Jewish Marriage Education

Established with the encouragement & guidance of Maran Hagaon Rabbi **Shlomo Zalman Auerbach** zt"l
In consultation with Maran Hagaon Rabbi **Yosef Sholom Elyashiv** zt"l

JME International: POB 43206 Jerusalem, 91431 Israel Tel: 972-8-974-1030 Fax: 972-8-976-0914
www.JewishFamily.org   info@jewishfamily.org

✳ Jewish Marriage Education (JME) is a non profit international organization dedicated to bringing a deeper understanding of marriage and family life according to Torah to the Jewish community.

✳ The organization conducts lectures and counselor training classes worldwide according to a curriculum approved by Gedolei Yisrael, the highest rabbinical authorities.

✳ These counselors are equipped to teach and review the essence of the Jewish marriage and the laws and insights into Taharat Hamishpachah to bridegrooms and married men and brides and married women.

✳ JME also publishes and distributes educational material pertaining to the Jewish home which includes:

> ✳ **Books**
>
> **The Secret of Jewish Femininity** - Insights into the Practice of Taharat HaMishpachah
>
> **Two Halves of a Whole -** Torah Guidelines for Marriage
>
> **Straight from the Heart -** A Torah Perspective on Mothering through Nursing
>
> **Our Family, Our Strength -** Creating a Jewish Home
>
> **The Unique Princess -** Understanding the Significance of Modesty in Building the Jewish Home
>
> ✳ **The books may be obtained also in other languages**
>
> ✳ **Harmony in the Home -**
> A unique program of character improvement for parents and children which includes - a musical disc with songs and stories by Reb Alter, an illustrated book and a full color motivational chart.
>
> ✳ **Discs and booklets on the subjects of Taharat HaMishpachah, Shalom Bayit, Parenting and Modesty.**
>
> ✳ **The Married Woman's Complete Personal Kit which includes:**
> A personal calendar
> A perpetual sunset calendar
> A checklist and prayer card
> A pretty pouch for personal cloths
> High quality personal cloths

For further information, for referral to a counselor and for ordering educational material:

JME International: POB 43206 Jerusalem, 91431 Israel Tel: 972-8-974-1030 Fax: 972-8-976-0914
www.JewishFamily.org   info@jewishfamily.org